# THE GARDENS

A Ghost Story

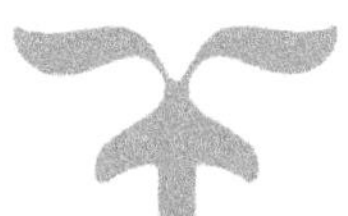

haroldstraugh@copyright2023

# Chapters

# Introduction

The year was 1987, ten years after The Gardens had opened its doors. For its time, the Gardens was considered one of the top retirement homes in Indiana.  With its massive greenhouse, artwork in the main lobby, colored T.V.'s in all the rooms, state-of-the-art beds, and actual chefs to cook the meals.

The lobby itself was something to be admired.  It was an A-frame in structure with two large windows on each side of the entrance door, that stretched two stories high.  There was a black and white, marble countertop that acted as a receptionist desk to the right of the entrance doors when someone first walked it.  There were red, suede couches and bear-claw chairs for people to sit on.  A large, square, wood panel T.V. was there for everyone's entertainment.

Employees and new admits would go down a long hall to the back, left of the receptionist desk to an elevator that would take them down to the rooms.  Once off the elevator they'd travel up a long corridor, with cinderblock walls, painted a light, hunter green. The flooring was a thin, floral carpet, then came a set of double doors that employees had to use a badge to open.  Once inside, the floor slightly elevated, there were walnut, handrails on both sides of the hall.

Then came the hall that housed the rooms, facing east and west each hall had sixteen rooms to it. Each room had its own bed, thick, tan, orange, and black carpet, either the resident's personal beds, or a bed provided by the retirement home, a small kitchen, and a main bathroom with various pastel-colored tiles.  Some rooms were three bedrooms and some had two. Facing each hall, the rooms on the west side, on the left and the rooms on the east side on the right, including the main dining room all had a glorious view of the garden, the pride and joy of the building.

The greenhouse that housed the garden was a magnificent, glorious, crystal-clear glass dome that covered the backside and outside of the building.  When inside, it looked as if it towered over the building, but from the outside the top of the dome, was just half a story above ground.

Inside the greenhouse were plants of many types, perennials, annuals, small trees, a large viewing pond with a catwalk from one side to the other. The pond had a small waterfall on the north end and was filled with coy fish.  Apple trees surrounded the pond so the residents could enjoy a snack as they roamed around the massive garden.  The entry way to the massive garden was at the end of the west hall, the doors were kept open during the day and locked up by the night security guard and opened in the morning.

Speaking of the security guard there, he had been there from the minute the doors opened.  He picked up the name Jingling Jim McCurdy because his keys would always jingle when he walked.  He was a tall, slender man, pale as could be, cold grey eyes and bad teeth, with both canines missing.  He kept a sloppily, trimmed beard and despite looking evil with his cold, grey eyes, and arched eyebrows, he started out one of the nicest people that the residents loved.  That all changed over time and soon the evilness that was Jingling Jim McCurdy came through.  One of the residents came up with poem about him, "Jingling Jim McCurdy, does the residents dirty." That poem took off like a wildfire and that resident was, the first of many residents to disappear under Jim's watch.

# Chapter One: The Wrath of Jingling Jim McCurdy

It was late one summer night in June 1987, the ten-year anniversary party was wrapping up and no one invited Jingling Jim McCurdy.  The employees and residents enjoyed a nice dinner and door prizes as Jingling Jim McCurdy enjoyed a cigarette and beer from his Ford Pinto in the parking lot.  He took a long drag from the cigarette, blew the smoke out of his nose as he chugged the beer.

He got out of his car, flipped his cigarette at another car and watched as it lit up a bright orange upon impact.  He then took his beer can, crushed the blue and white can and threw it as hard as he could.  It bounced off the pavement and hit another car in parking lot.

The air was thick with humidity as he walked from the back-parking lot to the front door.  He ran his hand through his short, wavy, salt and pepper hair, "Guess it's time to get this shit-show going," he said and opened the door.  There wasn't a receptionist that time of night, so he headed straight to the elevator.

The elevator was painted tan and was nice when the place first opened, but had worn down over time. It was more like a freight elevator, the doors shut horizontally instead of vertically. Jingling Jim pressed the worn-down arrow button that lit up a dull yellow.  The elevator made a large clanking noise and Jingling Jim watched as a light lit up in the rectangular window, and a dinging noise came to ear, signaling the arrival of the elevator. The doors lifted, slapping against the top and bottom of the elevator.

"Piece of shit!" Jingling Jim said as he boarded the elevator. He pressed the down button and the doors started to shut, then stopped.  Jingling Jim reached up and grabbed the door by the lip of the door and tried pulling it down.  At first it didn't budge then, suddenly it gave and slammed shut and Jingling Jim fell to the floor,

"Goddammit!" he shouted. He got up and dusted his blue jeans off and waited for the elevator to open.

The doors opened and Jingling Jim could see the remainder of the people in the main dining room, "Damn idiots," he said as he opened the door just to the right of the elevator. It was the security office, it was a small, square, cinderblock room. The paint was a blue pastel and was flaking in spots. There were three, white, blocky, square computers with images from the outside of the building and the lobby. There was a white and fake wood paneled coffee pot and a small, fake wood paneled fridge with a silver handle. Jingling Jim kept his sodas and coffee in there.

The clock-in clock was right beside the door. Jingling Jim looked at the clock above the monitors, grabbed his off-white clock in sheet, lined up the slots and pulled the handle down. He pulled his card out and looked at it, "11 o'clock on the dot."

He was usually on time to make his first round, but people were taking longer to leave than normal, so Jingling Jim lit up a cigarette and puffed on it with his feet up on his desk. He watched as people exited out the lobby, then got up and went back up to lock the doors, flipping off the people as they walked away. As he walked by the marble countertop, he put his cigarette out on it, then flipped the butt behind the counter. He made a right at the opposite hall that led to the elevator.

A faded exit sign hung above the door that led to the outside. Jingling Jim walked around the outside of the dome looking down at the garden, but paying close attention to the rose garden. He smiled as he looked at the rose garden, because the rose garden was where Mr. John Luther was buried. Jingling Jim knew that because he buried him there. Mr. Luther was the resident that came up with the poem one night, and a year before, while the nurse went to break, Jingling Jim put a pillow over Mr. Luther's head and didn't remove it until his feet stopped moving.

He left Mr. Luther in his room and waited until his two-a.m. trash run and put Mr. Luther's body in a large, grey trash barrel and then went to the trash cans out in the garden. The foliage was thick enough to hide Jingling Jim from the view of the dining room as he dug a hole big enough to put Mr. Luther in and covered him up.  The very next night, Jingling Jim brought in rose seeds and planted them, they've grown ever since.  Also, ever since then, Jingling Jim was on a killing spree.

He drowned Mrs. Robison in one of the communities, whirlpools, and took her to the incinerator.  He drowned Mr. Jacobson in the pond and used the grey trash barrel to take him outside where there was a river nearby that he dumped him in.  It was anger that had been building up in him over the years of disrespect.  He knew the only way to get away from the disrespect was to get away from The Gardens, but he was a fifty-five-year-old, with bad knees and back, he was afraid he couldn't be hired anywhere.  He snapped back to reality and stared at the roses a little longer before finishing his round.

He went around to a shed that had axes, a mower and some other tools and small machinery for the lawn care around there.  He checked the lock, then headed back inside. He headed down to the end of the east hall, where there was a hallway to the left that led down to the kitchen. He checked the office doors there to make sure they were locked and left. He went back in the office and looked at the monitors once more.  He then left the office and headed down the double doors that led to the garden.  He locked them and double checked them to make sure no one could get in like Mr. Jacobson had done and threatened to turn him in for forgetting his job.  He then walked back to the dining room and shut all the curtains that revealed the garden when opened.

"Maybe I want them open," he heard the nightshift nurse Lucy say.  Lucy was a from the Philippines, though short in stature, her thought on how much authority she had, was taller than anything Jingling Jim had ever seen.

"I close them every night at midnight, like I've done for the last ten years Lucy, I tell you this all the time."

"I'll just open them back up once you leave," she said and walked away.

"Bitch!" Jingling Jim whispered and went about closing the curtains.

Things went smoothly for Jingling Jim until three o'clock. He was watching the cameras when he saw the night shift CNA, Mikayla, go unlock the lobby doors and let in a man, then they both sat on the couch.

"Damn that idiot!" he said to himself and headed to the elevator.

He got in and went to the lobby and when the doors opened, Mikayla and the man looked shocked. Mikayla was dressed in a white dress, her blonde hair pulled back with a red and white stripped piece of fabric. Mikayla was well built and usually perked her chest out when anyone came around. The man was wearing a black, leather jacket, he had his hair slicked back, with a slight curl up front and cigarette in his mouth. His was muscular, Jingling Jim could tell from his square, jawline that was slightly sunken in on the sides and brown, wide eyes.

"Mikayla, you can't unlock those doors and let people in," Jingling Jim snapped.

"Calm down my man, she ain't hurting nothing," the man said.

"It's against the rules and I'm the one who suffers for it when they're broken," Jingling Jim said, his face grew flushed.

The man adjusted his collar on his leather jacket and squirmed around a little.  Lightning struck outside in the distance causing Mikayla to jump, "Look, why don't you go get a real job? Like a real man instead of harassing people," the man said then flipped his cigarette at Jingling Jim's face.  It missed his right eye by a fraction of an inch.

Jingling Jim reeled back in pain and took off to the nearest restroom which was straight back in the center of the hall the leads either outside or to the elevator.  He raced in and turned on the light, which flickered and hummed.  He looked at where the cigarette hit and it burned a circle through his eyebrow and slightly scorched his skin.

"A real job?  A REAL JOB?" Jingling Jim asked himself, "What would that greaser know about a real job? He probably can't even wipe his own ass without mommy's help."

It was then all the years of disrespect from the nurses and residents, came crashing down on him.  He flashbacked to about everything negative said to him, he needed to teach them all a lesson and the ones he couldn't teach that night was lucky.  The light flickered a few more times as Jingling Jim stared into his own, cold, grew eyes in the mirror before he snapped out of it and left the bathroom to head outside.

"Later, loser!" the man said as Jingling Jim headed to the door that led outside. Jingling Jim said nothing, just stared for a second and went outside. It was raining, but it felt good to Jingling Jim as he walked up to the shed and unlocked it.  He went in removed the axe and hedge trimmers, he put the scissor-like hedge trimmers, through a belt loop causing them to slightly sag to the side.  He then put the axe shaft on his shoulder and had a sinister smile on his face.

He walked up to the main entrance from the outside and looked in, Mikayla and the man she let in, were on a couch, with their backs facing the main entrance.  Jingling Jim put his keys in his pocket, to help muffle the sound and slowly opened the door.  He then walked slowly, raising the axe way above his head and when he was about three feet away from the man, he brought the axe down.

He sunk the blade a good six inches into the man's head, a cracking noise was heard as the blade smashed through the skull. Mikayla jumped and screamed, that's when Jingling Jim took the trimmers and tried cutting off Mikayla's head with them.  He failed, the blade only managed to cut through the soft tissue, hitting Mikayla's neck and kicking back.  He did silence her scream though. Mikayla grabbed for her throat as blood sprayed across Jingling Jim, the man, the couch, and the floor.  Jingling Jim removed the axe from the man, who then fell over sideways, blood and brain matter oozing out of the wound.  Jingling Jim, then took the axe and finished removing the head of Mikayla. There was mark on the floor where the axe hit after it passed through Mikayla's vertebrae.

Thunder struck again outside as Jingling Jim held up Mikayla's head and then kissed her dead lips, "You always were a doll-face," he said, then dropped the head, it bounced with a wet, squishing noise, then rolled slightly away from the body.  Blood spewed out from Mikayla's body a good four feet before slowing.  Jingling Jim walked through the blood puddle, leaving a trail of size, ten-and-a-half-wide shoeprints from the body to the elevator.

On the ride down, Jingling Jim had a smile on his face, and a cigarette in the corner of his mouth.  When he got off the elevator, no one was in sight, so he took the axe to the buttons, so no one could press them to get out. They sparked and the dull yellow lights, went black.  The elevator was the only way out and Jingling Jim made sure no one was leaving, including him.

He noticed movement in the far corner of the dining room and then the curtains flew open. Lucy was going to be his next victim. She was too busy messing with the curtains to notice Jingling Jim sneaking up on her.  He brought the axe up, just as she got the curtains open and she caught his reflection in the window and turned around. All she had time to do was gasp, as the axe sunk deep in her skull, right between her eyes. Her eyes crossed as they focused on the blade, a thin trail of blood came out both sides of the blade, almost looking like bloody tears as they streaked down her face.

Lucy fell to the ground as Jingling Jim held onto the axe, then put his foot on her chest and wiggled the blade loose from Lucy's face then went to fire up the incinerator.

The incinerator was located down the west hall, off to the right of the double doors that led to the garden.  It was mostly used for trash, but Jingling Jim had something more sinister in mind that night.  It was ten feet long, and five-feet tall, made of iron. The door was slotted so once lit Jingling Jim could feed smaller pieces of trash into it without opening the door.  Jingling Jim threw in a few pieces of wood that he kept for kindling, grabbed a torch, and lit the kindling, then threw in the trash.  He emptied out the trash cart and stuck it out in the hall.  He then used his keys to enter the resident's rooms and violently whack each one to the death.

He put their body parts in the trash cart then went on to each room.  Soon, blood started oozing out the bottom of the cart by the wheels, streaking the hallway with blood.  Even though screams filled the air, the residents couldn't get out of bed fast enough to elude fate.

After the incinerator was full, Jingling Jim tossed some body parts into the pond, then went back to the incinerator and stirred some of the body parts around so they would burn better.  He then went from room to room with his torch and started torching the rooms.  After he was done, he made, what would be his final trip to the incinerator.

Jingling Jim was stirring the bodies once more and added a few body parts to the fire.  He watched as they burned down and then, suddenly, he was shoved from behind and forced into the incinerator. The culprit was the dayshift maintenance man named, Rico. Jingling Jim had lost track of time and it was time to switch shifts.

The elevator was disabled from the ground floor, but the buttons still worked in the lobby.  After Rico found the dead bodies of Mikayla and her man, in the lobby, he phoned the police and went down without a second thought.  He was first to see the wrath Jingling Jim McCurdy had put on The Gardens. Rico proceeded with caution down the hall after hearing a door shut.  The door that shut was the door leading to the incinerator room, when he opened it, he saw even more horrors and acted quick.  He shoved Jingling Jim in and shut the incinerator's door.  He heard Jingling Jim scream out as he made a round to look for residents.  There were none living, so he ran to the highest part of the of dome on the inside next to the catwalk, busted a window out and made his escape as the police arrived.

The fires were too widespread by the time the firetruck arrived.  The only part that could be saved was the lobby, even with the rains help.  The police took Rico's statement. The Gardens was a total loss and after the multiple lawsuits from the families, the owners, The Puttlesmiths, were never able to recover financially.

The Gardens was condemned, but never torn down. It became a haunting figure on the backroads of Yertzville between Franklin and Edinburgh, Indiana.  Trees grew up all around it and it became a popular tourist attraction for avid ghost hunters, it wasn't until thirty-one years later when someone by the name of Mr. Helsir bought the property and decided to rebuild The Gardens.  It took three years, a grand re-opening and a job fair that was in late September 2018.

# Chapter Two: The Grand Reopening

It was a hot September day, the temperatures were reaching well into the nineties.  The Gardens had been completely rebuilt.  The owner, Mr. Helsir who sat in his limousine, with the windows rolled up, hosted a job fair. He was expecting, with all the hype, that more people would have showed up, but there was mere thirty people.

He arranged for booths with applications, popcorn, drinks, keychains, coozies anything to catch people's eyes.  He spared no expense, even so more, on the building itself.

The dome was completely redone, reinforced, double pane glass that couldn't be broken.  There were lights and heating system installed so the residents could enjoy the garden all year round. Fresh sod was put down inside and outside and Mr. Helsir had a company for the past three years, fertilizing it.

The lobby was still an A-frame, but with sliding doors, a semi-circular drive with a fountain in the middle.  The fountain was in the shape of an angel with her arms outstretched towards the sky and the water came out of her mouth.  There were LED lights installed and the fountain lit up different colors at night.

Inside the lobby, the marble countertop was replaced with a white, black, and gold speckled, granite countertop. The flooring was an epoxy paint that matched the theme of the countertop. The best, back-support chairs were put behind the receptionist counter.  A large, brushed-brass chandelier hung in the middle of the room. Two, black couches and three, off white chairs, filled the lobby for sitting.  The bathroom was taken out and two were added, right off the lobby.  The urinals and toilets were all auto-flush and the faucets were motion activated.

The freight elevator was redone and the doors put on the opposite way, the cable pulley was replaced with hydraulics, speakers were installed and soft, piano music played in it all hours of the night.

The carpet right off the elevator was replaced with a hunter green carpet and the walls painted a nice tan. The security office was gutted and three monitors were replaced and showed fourteen different cameras from around the building.  There was a refrigerator/microwave combo in the corner, and a set of four, light blue lockers.

The main dining room was done in a nice, white, black, and gold speckled tile with twenty, round tables and four chairs to each table.  The main dining room had recessed lighting that was dimmable for various lighting effects and a large chandelier.  The curtains were operated by a remote on the wall.

The rooms were all extended into three-room apartments. There was a bigger kitchen area, a nice countertop that divided the kitchen from the living room, a nook in the far-left corner that could be used for a dining room table.  A full-sized refrigerator, under-the-cabinet microwave and dishwasher were all luxuries that Mr. Helsir wanted for the residents.  The showers were walk-in but had sitting area and the shower heads were multiple shower heads in one.  Each apartment had two bathrooms, one in the right corner in the front room, and one in the master bedroom.  There were also emergency phones located in all bedrooms that would ring straight to nurse's station.

The garden was redone from the ground up.  As mentioned before, fresh sod was put down inside the dome to give it a more outside-like feel.  Various raised gardens were added, but no matter how anyone tried to get rid of the roses, they always regrew.  The pond was extended, the catwalk raised and a larger waterfall added.  There were two, offset sitting areas on the catwalk, were residents could sit and enjoy the sounds of the waterfall and watch the coy fish below. There was a built-in watering system, that periodically watered the plants.

Back at the job fair, Mr. Helsir still looked on with disappointment from his limousine. He was in his mid-fifties, and The Gardens was his life-long obsession. It was breaking his heart to see that not many people were there.  He motioned for his driver to leave.  The limousine drove away slowly, leaving the job fair to the Human Resource Department, that's what they were hired for.

At the end of the day the Human Resource Department had a total of fifteen applications. James, the head of Human Resources, tossed the applications down on his desk. James was tall and skinny, with a bald head and thin, wire-glasses.  He had a bump in the middle of his nose which caused the tip of his nose to point down.  He had a scar on his lower left lip and always had stubble but never a full mustache.

The Human Resource Department was located behind a door, behind the receptionist desk.  As he tossed the applications down, one fell off on the floor and James picked it up and looked at it. The name on top of the application was Richard Ruiz.

# Chapter Three: Richard Ruiz

Richard Ruiz was a five-foot-four, one-hundred-and-twenty-pound man whose mother and father originated from Guatemala. He was about four when his dad went to work one day and never came home, instead his dad was committed to a nearby insane asylum.

Richard's mom raised him the best she could, so when he was of age to work, he wanted to help his mom out.  He found most jobs somewhat hard because of his short stature but he got by.  He finally worked his way into security but got laid off, so it was perfect timing that the job fair popped up around the time he had gotten laid off.

Richard was sitting at the table with his mom, who was just a little shorter than him.  She had long black hair that was pulled into a ponytail and braided.  She had, unfortunately, a very square jawline, bushy, black eyebrows, dark skin and beady eyes.  She always looked angry but was one the nicest people in Yertzville.  He was looking at the newspaper as they were eating tamales and tacos.

"Hey mom, they have an opening at The Gardens, night-time security, eleven to seven. They have a job fair tomorrow, I might go," he said and took a bite from one of the beef tamales, he dipped it into a red, chipotle sauce and took another bite.

Mrs. Ruiz was mid-bite through a taco, when her son asked about The Gardens, she stopped chewing and swallowed.  The taco shell cut the inside of her throat on way down, small tears formed in her eyes.  She was frozen in fear as she looked at her son.  She couldn't reveal what she knew about the place, it would reveal too much to Richard.  His eyes were sparkling and he was smiling, she hadn't seen that in a few days.  She had hoped the demons of The Gardens' past were gone.

"I think you should give it shot, I know you love being a security officer," she said nervously drank some sweet tea.

"I will go in the morning momma and hopefully I will get some good news for a change," Richard said and scarfed down another tamale.

"I will say a prayer tonight, God will be on your side."

"I hope so momma, it'd be nice if he had my back," Richard said, gaining a narrowed look from his mom.

"You know better than to doubt the good lord," Mrs. Ruiz said.

The rest of the meal was in silence.  Richard took and cleaned up, washed the dishes, and put them away.  He then mopped the floor while his mom rested.  She took care of the home for so many years, it was his turn.

The house he lived in with his momma wasn't the biggest, it was a two-bedroom, two bath home, with a spacious living room and kitchen. It was dated, the light fixtures were still brass, the tile on the kitchen floor was a faded yellow, the carpet everywhere else was tan. The bathrooms still had blue tiles in the showers, but was never removed for fear of asbestos.

The outside had a light blue, vinyl siding, with white trim around the windows.  It was ranch style in shape, but no garage and a driveway, that had a few cracks in it.  The driveway was lined with hedges that Richard would trim down once a week.

Richard took a shower, set the alarm on his phone, and then went to bed.  He was so nervous he didn't sleep much and was up before his alarm.  He combed his short, curly, black hair with a coarse, horse-hair brush.  He put on black dress pants and a black, polo shirt. He took his golden Saint Christopher, kissed it, and put it on, he then put on a white, wide-brimmed ball cap. He trimmed up his short, beard and smiled.  He then headed outside and got on his bike, he kept the car there if his momma needed it.

The Gardens was only about half a mile away from his house, it was set out in the country, but could easily be seen from U.S. 31. As he rode, he was passing banners announcing the job fair.  They were yellow, ten feet tall and flapped in the wind, so much Richard could hear them was he rode by on his bike.

Richard spotted The Gardens and he stopped on his bike for a second to admire it, "Holy shit!" he said to himself.  He could see a few tents set up on the outside, but the building is what caught his eye the most.  He continued to pedal and after a few more minutes he turned down the driveway that led to The Gardens.  He parked his black, ten speed off onto the grass, so there was plenty of room for cars.

Richard instantly started regretting wearing black, luckily, he remembered to put on deodorant as he came up to the first blue and white canopy tent.  There was a short, long blonde hair and blue-eyed girl with a slight tan named Sheila.  She was peppy and had the whitest smiles of all times, her voice was quiet and somewhat mousey.  Her looks fooled everyone, she was a hunter and damn good one at that.

"Good morning! How are you?" she asked Richard as he walked up to her tent.  She had applications, coozies, bottle openers, key chains, and pens.

"I'm doing good, I heard you have a position open for night security?" Richard asked.

"We do! It's Monday-Friday or Sat-Sun, we would like to fill both positions immediately.  Now, it's not just security, you do light janitorial, clean carpets and mop and wax the lobby and dining room. There will be a schedule on your first day, but ultimately, you can you use your own discretion and modify it to your likings.  You have a trash run at one and four a.m., then at five-thirty you unlock the lobby.  I know it's more of glorified janitor job with a tagline of security, but I hope that doesn't dissuade you from applying."

"No ma'am, I need a job and I can't be picky right now. I'm simply curious, what's the pay?"

"That's the good part, they pay you a security wage instead of a janitor wage, so it'll be eighteen an hour starting out with a ten percent raise at the end of your first year," Sheila looked at Richard like she just delivered a deal breaker to him.

"That's four more dollars than what I was making. Is there a place I can fill this out?" Richard asked.

"Yes, there's a table and chair," she pointed to a lone table and a chair, that Richard had somehow overlooked, "Here take a pen, then turn it in to James over at the other tent," she then pointed to another tent, where a man, who was tall, skinny and bald, was looking rather annoyed.

Richard went and sat down, taking the blue pen, with gold letters on it that read "The Gardens".  The pen wrote smooth for looking rather cheaply made.  Richard scribbled down his address, previous job experiences and what few references he had.  He wiped the sweat from his brow before it dripped on his application.  He signed and dated it, then walked over to James and turned it in. James took it and hastily tossed it down.

"Thank you, if we're interested, we will call you," James said and that was it.

Richard got back on his bike and rode home.  He shed the black clothes and put on some shorts and short-sleeved shirt.  He went straight to mowing the grass to keep his mind busy from thinking about the application.  He wouldn't hear about it for three more days.

## **Chapter Four: The call, the training**

## **and the questions**

It was a late afternoon, Richard was busy with his typical housework, stressing about the upcoming bills when his phone rang. He had forgotten to save The Gardens number in his phone, but he didn't know anyone that would call him, so he answered.

"Hello?" Richard asked.

"Is this Richard Ruiz?" he heard a man's voice ask.

"Yes, it is!"

"This is James Smerns from The Gardens, I was calling regarding your application. I was wanting to set up a time for some training, mostly on routine, show you the building and run through on the carpet cleaners if you have time this week, that would be great," James said.

"Yes, I do have time, plenty of time, any day this week," Richard said.

"Well, Friday would be the best time, of course it would be during that day, start time would be seven in the morning and we would stop at three. It would be paid training of course."

"Yes, that sounds good, I will see you bright and early Friday morning." Richard said with a big smile on his face.

"Okay," James said and hung up the phone, not sharing Richard's enthusiasm.

"HEY MOMMA!" Richard yelled.

"WHAT? I'M WATCHING MY SHOWS, THIS BETTER BE IMPORTANT, OR YOU GET THE CHANCLETAS!" his mom, Maria yelled back from the front room.

"I GOT THE JOB, I HAVE TRAINING FRIDAY!"

"THAT'S GOOD NEWS, NOW SHUT UP, YOU'RE RUINING MY SHOW!" Maria said and laughed.

Richard said nothing more after that, just smiled and kissed his Saint Christopher, "I knew I could trust in you."

Two days later, Richard was up and riding his bike at six-thirty in the morning. He wore khaki pants and a white dress shirt. He knew he would be inside most the day, so he wasn't worried about getting too hot, just nervous. He parked his bike in a bike rack that was located next to the main entrance and he stepped up to the doors and his future opened in front of him.

He walked up to the granite countertop, behind it was an older lady, with a bob-style haircut, long in the front, short in the back. She had on blue eyeshadow, and her eyelids were slightly droopy, but her green eyes were bright. She was in her late sixties, wearing bright, overdone, red lipstick that covered her once plump lips but now sagged in the corners no matter how hard she smiled. Her earrings were too small for the holes they were in and sagged as well. She would often forget what she was doing. Her name was Lola, and she smiled when Richard walked in.

"Hello, how can I help you today?" she said, her voice a little crackly.

"I'm here to meet James for orientation," Richard said and smiled.

"Okay, once sec, I'll phone him and let you know he's here," she said.

"You mean let him know I'm here?" Richard asked, catching her mistake.

"Yes dear, that's what I said," Lola said and picked up the phone.  She pressed a few buttons and waited, "Yes James, your seven o'clock is here. Yes! It is nice he is early," she said then hung up the phone, "He will be with you in second."

Richard nodded and no sooner he went to turn to sit down, a door opened up from behind the desk and out stepped James wearing a tight, blue shirt, white pants and tan, leather shoes, holding an iced coffee in a clear cup.  He took big sip of the coffee, making an annoying slurping noise as he done so.

"I'll have you come back here and fill out the boring paperwork, then we will get started, there's coffee back here if you want some!" James said and motioned for Richard to follow him behind the door.

There was a section between the receptionist desk and a wall, that housed a swinging door.  Richard pushed it opened and it gave an odd squeak as he walked through it and went through the door behind the desk.

There was a hallway about twenty feet long with doors on each side, equally down the hall and a third door at the end of the hall.  The door at the end of the hall was a dark mahogany with a black handle. The two other doors weren't so dark and had brushed, bronze handles.  The door on the right was open and the one on the left was closed and Richard noticed Sheila's name on the door as he passed. James led Richard to the door at the back of the hallway.

Once through the door, there was large room with grey painted walls, and a large, brown, oval table in the middle of the room, but it only had three chairs.  There was a stack of papers on the table and one of those cheap pens.  To the right of the table, there was single-cup coffee maker and various kinds of coffee.  The room had a distinct smell of pineapple and sage, which caught Richard a little off guard.

"Coffee is over there and this is just the typical paperwork for employment.  Name, date of birth, social security number, your soul, you know, they typical stuff," James said and laughed, "Just bring it down to my office when you're done but first a picture," James said and broke out his phone and snapped a picture, "I'll have your name badge shortly."

James disappeared from the room, leaving Richard to himself, in the odd smelling room.  Richard picked up the pen and started to fill out the paperwork, page after page of information, then an aptitude test.  He got up halfway through the test and looked at the variety of coffees but noticed a green tea and decided to take it.  He added two sugars and went back to the paperwork.

He was just finishing up when he heard a whisper.  He stopped and looked around and no one was in the room.  He figured he heard something from Sheila or James.  He signed his name and as soon as he put the date, he heard a whispered, "Weeeellllllcoooome!"

"Oh thank you!" he said without looking up.

"Who are you talking to?" he looked up and saw Sheila standing there.

A look of confusion came over Richard's face, "You didn't just say "Welcome!" to me?"

"No! I was just seeing how you were doing and if you had any questions?"

"Just one, who said "Welcome!"?" he laughed, "I'm all done."

"Okay, turn it into James and I'll be taking you on your tour and giving you the run down around the place," Sheila smiled.

"Sounds good."

"I'll meet you in the lobby," she said her blue eyes gleaming at Richard.

Sheila left and Richard gathered up his paperwork. He walked down to James's office and turned them in. James handed him a plastic card, with his picture on it, and title "Night Security". "I need you try that out at the card readers. It'll let you in all the closets, the monitor room, which will essentially just be your room, the side dock for trash, so on and so on. The only place it won't let you in, is the med-room, you don't need to be in there anyways."

Richard took the name badge and with the aid of clip, attached it to his shirt and flipped it with his finger. He then went into the lobby and Sheila was waiting for him by one of the big chairs.

"If you want to follow me to the exit sign, we will try your badge there and see if it unlocks the door."

Richard followed Sheila, who was wearing tight, tan capris, white tennis shoes, a tan, jean jacket and white shirt. She had her blonde hair pulled into a ponytail, with a matching, tan hair clip. They walked up to the door to the back right of the desk, with a large exit sign above it. To the right of the door was a little black box with a small blue light on the top right corner.

"Put your badge up to that and see if the light turns green," Shelia pointed to the card reader. Richard put his badge up to it and it beeped, then the light turned from blue to green and a clicking sound came from the door and he was able to push it open.

"Now, right over there," she pointed to large, metal, brown container with a door on the side and a green and red button next to the door, "is where you take the trash every night. Now, let's try the elevator."

They walked opposite the door that led to the trash compactor.  There was the elevator the would lead below, redone and reimaged.  The stainless-steel doors were freshly cleaned the night before.  The card reader was to the left, right next to the push buttons.  Richard scanned his badge and the pressed the down-arrow button.  A loud "DING!" came to ear as the stainless-steel doors slid open.  They both got in and Sheila pressed the down button.

The elevator moved and then a second later, the doors opened, revealing the long, slightly inclined hallway.  Richard could see the massive chandelier that illuminated the main dining room from down by the elevator.  Richard didn't care too much for the swirly pattern of the carpet, but he ignored it.  There was a door to the right, that had a card reader.

"That's technically your office. There will be a weekend guy here, but you won't see him and he won't see you, he won't have the duties you do, mostly just trash runs and keeping an eye on the place.  Go ahead and try your badge here as well."

Richard tried his badge and the door opened.  He entered the room and noticed the monitors.  There were four screens with numerous cameras, with colored pictures throughout the building. There were so many angles, so many different things to look at. Then a small square clock, with digital number pad that Sheila said was where he clocked in at.  There was a large chair in front of the desk, with arm rest and Richard noticed some type of battery box at the back of the chair.

"What's that?" he asked and pointed to it.

"Oh, that chair is a heated, massage chair. There is a fridge and microwave combo over there and some lockers.  The desk is stocked with pens and notepaper.  There will be maintenance men during the day, but their office is across the hall. Your badge won't work for them, and theirs won't work for yours.  If you get a call at night that bulb is out, you change the bulb, if that doesn't work, you grab a pink ticket, on the corner of the desk," she pointed, "and write it up, then put it in their slot on their door. You will see some of the maintenance men in the morning, thirty-minutes before you clock out."

"You can pass along anything and they might ask you questions.  Of course the first couple of weeks it'll just be getting routines and getting to know your co-workers."

"I understand, but I'm left alone pretty much?"

"Yeah, the stuff described shouldn't take too long. On nights you just have trash runs, you will have free time, you can make rounds if you want.  I know waxing and buffing the dining room and lobby will take time, you have to move all the tables and chairs into the closet, but you only have to start to get them back out.  It's actually dayshifts job to finish them before eight." Sheila said, for jobs that hadn't been worked before, she had a good idea on how they were supposed to go.

"Now if you would like to follow me, I will show you the nurse's station, the dining room, our model room of what the residents room looks like, then the main attraction, the garden. Then I'll show you where we keep the carpet, tile cleaners and wax, I assume you know how to use those?"

"I've done this before yes, of course every machine is different, but I'm a quick learner.  I can spend my downtime learning the machines," Richard said to show he was fully capable of doing the job regardless of lack of knowledge.

"I like you, you show ambition," Sheila smiled and started walking up the ramp to the nurse's station and main dining room.

"We had some nurses pulled from other locations that Mr. Helsir operates, some are leaving when we find replacements, but one nightshift nurse is staying.  All sales are done at a different location.  This gave us the resources to get residents in here quickly.  Some have been here a few weeks before Mr. Helsir wanted to bring in fresh faces….incase you were wondering," Sheila spewed out.

"I wasn't, but the information is nice to know," Richard said as they walked across a split hallway to the nurse's station, which was set up like the receptionist desk.

It was half a square in shape, with a countertop to match the black, gold and white tile in the dining room. Thick glass, sixteen-feet long by four-feet high, that went from the top of the countertop to the ceiling, supported with one-inch-wide steel beams, every eight feet.  There was a door on the backside, that faced the dining room.  There was heavy-set nurse with her back towards the glass, looking at a computer.  There was a small, round, metal intercom in the middle of one of the glass panels. It was very old-school and Sheila caught Richard looking at it.

"That's the original intercom, it was the only thing the fire didn't destroy here back in eighty-seven."

"I've heard about that, but didn't know how true it was," Richard said and gleamed, he was paranormal fanatic.

"Unfortunately, we can't really talk about what happened back them, but they never said I couldn't deny what happened either," she smiled.

They entered the dining room, a massive chandelier hung in the middle with plenty of recessed lights in the ceiling.  Twenty round tables with chairs filled the dining room.  They were covered in floral table clothes, and chairs to match.  A huge, multi-sectional bay window, that exposed an excellent view of the garden, with the large waterfall, facing the dining room.

"That's really beautiful," Richard said.

"The residents really enjoy it. Over there is the closet that all the tables go into, they fold up and there is a chair dolly in there you can load the chairs up with. Now, I will take you down east hall, to the kitchen, you won't have too much to do in there, except trash run. They're responsible for mopping the floors and they have their own maintenance."

He followed Sheila down east hall.  The halls were wide enough for three people to walk side-by-side.  The doors to the rooms were solid oak, with brass room numbers on them.  There was a solid oak banister for the residents to grab onto.  The numbers on the door on east hall were all even numbers.  They went all the way down the hall to an open room that had two chairs and took a left.

"Use your badge to see if it lets you in the kitchen," Sheila said.

Richard used his badge and the double doors swung outwards, "Now down there is a ramp to the outside, that is used for kitchen deliveries, the elevator, stairs and this ramp are the only ways out of here.  You'll have to check the doors leading out to the ramp on your nightly rounds.  Whenever you use your badge, it time stamps so we know what time you made the round."

"Very stalkerish," Richard said and garnered a chuckle from Sheila.

They walked through the double doors and the hunter green, floral carpet turned to brown tile with thick black grout. There was a soda pop machine right past the entrance.  They walked down a small hall, with white walls and the hallway opened to a large room.  There were four double stoves, two-large flattop grills, three mixers, four back to back prep tables, three meat slicers and an array of knives on a magnetic strip.  There were people running around preparing meals and the phrase, "Yes Chef!" being yelled out a lot. One person, who wore a white chef's jacket, was calling out the orders.  He was medium height, man, who was incredible skinny, but had a smile that stretched across his face.

"Hi, Shelia!" the man said.

"Hi, Jason!" Shelia said, "That's our head chef, he's super nice and sometimes makes lunch for James and I."

Richard nodded to Jason and Jason went back to barking orders as Richard and Sheila walked by.  The two went back to the second set of double doors and without prompt, Richard used his badge to open them up.  They opened to a large storage room full of dry food and a set of freezers off to the right, and another set of double doors.  The room was cool forty degrees and was kept that way for preservation of the food.  They walked up to the last set of double doors and Richard tried his badge once again.  The doors opened to a steep loading ramp.

"I bet that's difficult to back down," Richard said.

"We've had issues but it's getting better," Sheila said and sighed, "Next we will go down west hall and show you where we keep the cleaning supplies."

They retraced their path and went down west hall, the numbers on west hall were all odd numbers.  They went to the end of the west hall, opposite the doors that led out the garden.  There was a door right next to an area that looked like a door used to be there.  That door took a set of keys, Sheila produced the key and opened the door.  Inside the room was a propane buffer, a large walk-behind floor scrubber, two carpet extractors, then the wax, floor stripper and cleaning supplies all up on the shelf, with foot booties hanging up on the wall. There was also a grey trash dumpster on wheels.

"What's with this?" Richard said and pointed to old door imprint on the wall.

"I don't know the whole story behind that, just heard they covered it up, because it used to lead to the old incinerator and few days later, the outline appeared, they tore it out and redone it and it came back, so they left it.

"Hmm, the incinerator," Richard said, he remembered reading an old newspaper article about the incinerator and how Jim McCurdy disposed of most his victims in it, but he knew not to bring it up.

"Now we go to the garden," Sheila's eyes lit up.

There was, once again a set of double doors, that needed badge entry, but also locked via Allen key.  They entered the garden and Richard stopped to admire the beauty.  It had its own atmosphere, a little heavy on the humidity, but was they walked up the catwalk, the coolness from the pond could be felt.  Richard noticed the rose garden right away.

"What's a little out of place," he said and pointed to the rose garden," he pointed to the roses.

"Yes, none of the gardeners hired said they planted them, but they look pretty and residents love them, so we kept them.  James should have your set of keys made up.  They're easy, you have a master key for east hall, and west hall.  You have an Allen key for garden doors and the main master key or GGMK as its stamped, that will get in you into the rest of the doors in case the badge system fails."

"I hope that doesn't happen," Richard said.

"It shouldn't, but technology is technology."

"True."

"Let's head back and see if James has your keys, ready."

They left the garden and headed back up to the lobby, James did have Richards keys ready, which were color coated, and gave him his time clock number. Then James asked Richard's shirt size, which was a medium, but Richard said large.  James disappeared in his office and came back out with an armful of grey shirts.

"You will have to buy pants to go with these, either grey or black and prefer you to have no-skid shoes, which we give you a voucher for," James said, then handed Richard an envelope.

"Oh, thank you!" Richard said the took the shirts.

"Your start time is Monday, ten-forty-five until seven, dayshift will be here at six-thirty, I'm sure Sheila explained that to you," James said.

"She did."

"Alright, here's the nightly schedule, you can take it home and study it, that way you're not struggling when you start, I mean, it will be a struggle until you get a routine."

"Will do," Richard said, "Do you have a bag I could put this in? I rode my bike, might be hard to carry," Richard asked.

"Oh sure thing, it even says The Gardens on it," James smiled and went back to his office to reappear a second later with green bag, that had The Gardens in golden letters.  Richard put the shirts and papers in the bag and headed on his way. A since of excitement came over his face as he pedaled home.

Monday night rolled around and Richard's alarm went off at eight-forty-five.  He got up, showered, put on his Saint Christopher, dressed in his work uniform, and headed to work.

The fountain was lit up beautifully at night and Richard smiled as he rode past it and put his bike up.  He wrapped a chain around it and put a lock through the two end pieces.  He walked up to the door and a man was standing there and let him in.

"You must be Richard," he said after letting Richard in.  He was a medium built man, with a little bit of belly, a trimmed, brown beard, balding, with glasses and beady, green eyes, "I'm Ron!" he said and stuck out his hand.

"I am Richard, how'd your first day go?" Richard asked.

"Not too bad, some of the residents are more dementia patients than not, I didn't know that, they're kind of trapped down here," Ron said as they walked towards the elevator.

"I didn't know that either, they seemed so lively when I was here the other day, so they're saying it's a retirement community, but it's more like a nursing home," Richard said.

"Pretty much," Ron said as he swiped his badge and the elevator opened and they went in. They rode down in silence.

When the doors opened Ron went to the door on the left, "I leave in thirty, they gave you a can of coffee for your first night, I'll knock when I'm ready to leave," Ron said.

Richard opened the door to his office and there on the desk as a large can of coffee with bow on it and fruit basket with some apples and oranges.  He made him a pot of coffee and opened the basket to grab an apple.  He took a bite of it and looked at the screens.  He watched as the second and third shift switched over and heard as many people walked by and get on the elevator.  He watched them on the screens as they exited the building and made their way into the parking lot.

A few minutes after watching everyone leave and having his office fill up with the smell of coffee, Ron knocked on his door. Richard got up and opened it and there stood Ron, with a black, clothlike, lunch pail in his hand.

"I'm ready if you are," Ron said, and the two went back up to the lobby.  Richard followed Ron out and up to the sliding doors where Ron instructed him on what to do, "You turn in to "Entrance Off" it'll shut, then you lock it.  If people need to come in after hours, they'll press a button that'll alarm you, we have the same set up in our shop."

Ron left and Richard followed Ron's directions and locked the door with his GGMK key, Richard then went back down to his office and looked at his list.  He was to make a round and check all locks at midnight.  So, he got back up and headed to the kitchen.  He checked the doors at the ramp, then went to the garden, he walked around the garden, admiring the roses, then locked the doors to the garden. He stopped on his way back and stared at the outline of the old door, it was faint but noticeable.

Richard got back to his office, and noticed a coffee cup that he had overlooked, once again, the colors green with gold letters came to play.  He poured himself a cup of coffee, straight black and set it aside to cool, and looked at the screens.  He went to take a bite out of the apple and a horrible taste filled his mouth.  He looked down at the apple in his hand, and it was filled with maggots.  He spit it out all over desk and tossed the apple down.  He wiped his mouth repeatedly, his face contorted in disgust and then looked again.  The apple was fine, there were no maggots on it or on his desk.

"Must be my nerves," he said as confusion set in, he took a sip of his coffee and then cleaned his desk.  He looked over at the screens and everything seemed alright so he looked at his list again. He wanted to learn the list so over time he'd just remember it.  It read for him to scrub the dining room with the walk-behind-floor scrubber.

He started walking up towards the dining room The nurse's station was to the right of the dining room before entering. He noticed the nurse at the nurse's station.  She was of African American descent, she had light brown eyes, plump lips, sleek face, and jawline.  Her eyebrows were high set, always looking surprised.  She waved at Richard as he walked by so Richard decided to stop.

"I'm Richard, how are you?" he asked through intercom.

"I'm Michelle, I'm doing fine, enjoying your first night?"

"Yes, you?"

"Learning the people, mostly they're asleep but I have meds and Cynthia starts waking them around six, if they requested it. They're mostly assisted living, a few have dementia, but nothing too bad."

"Cynthia? I haven't seen her yet," Richard said.

"She's probably doing room check, what are you doing?"

"I have to scrub the dining room, then shut the curtains, for some reason they want them shut and then opened at sunrise."

"Well, that sucks, I like watching the waterfall, but ya gotta do what ya gotta do," she said and turned her back to Richard to look at the computer screen.

Richard started walking down west hall and suddenly someone came out of a room and ran into him, "Oh shit, I'm sorry," he said.

"No, I'm sorry, I should have been looking, I'm Cynthia," she said. Cynthia was half Japanese, half white. She wasn't very tall, but she carried herself well and Richard briefly stared down at her breasts, which seemed too big for her body, but he looked away before she caught him. She was wearing beige scrubs with white tennis shoes. She had her hair pulled up in roll, clipped with a black, banana hair clip.

"I'm Richard, I'm the night security here."

"Well, it's nice to meet you, I have to go finish my room checks, I don't mean to be rude," she smiled.

"Not rude at all, I will talk at you later," Richard said and finally made it to the room that housed the cleaning machine.

The walk-behind scrubber was a large, blue machine that had an angled and rounded front, with a white squeegee on the back. There was a lever, halfway between the handle and the squeegee, that dropped the squeegee. It was plugged in, so Richard unplugged it from the machine. In between the handles was an on and off switch, a switch that lowered and raised the scrubbers and one that activated the squeegee. There was a water hose that was hanging above a sink basin on the floor. He filled the machine up and followed the instructions on the lid for the scrubber. He flipped it on and heard a click, then rotated the handle back and the machine moved towards him, he pulled it out in the hallway, then turned it around. It made a noticeable whine as he went down the hall.

He got to the dining room and moved half the tables over to the other side instead of putting them up like he was told, he then pressed the switch to lower scrubbers, activated and lowered the squeegee and scrubbed half the dining room. He moved everything from the unclean side and moved it back to the clean side. It took him well over an hour which made him late for his trash run, which Sheila and James left out on how to do.

He noticed when putting the scrubber back and grabbing the trash cart, there was a door that read "West Trash Room", he opened it and there were three, fifty-five-gallon trash cans, full of trash. He pulled them out, replaced the bags and headed down the hall.  As he was passing the nurse's station, Michelle tapped on the window and showed Richard a small but full trash bag. He walked around to the door and took it for her and she thanked him, he noticed Cynthia was behind the nurse's station as well.  He found a "East Trash Room" and repeated the process.  Then he went into the kitchen, but the trash was kept in the dry storage area, which struck Richard as unsanitary.  He shook his head and put the trash in the cart and headed back down east hallway, made a right and went to the elevator.

He went up and then headed to the door in the lobby that led outside and to the trash compactor. He used the built-in door stop that he pressed down with his foot to keep the door from shutting in the lobby. He walked to the trash compactor, the air was heavy with moisture and it made his shirt start to stick to him. He opened the door, and threw all the trash in the compactor.  He pressed a green button and listened as the compactor rumbled to life.  He watched as a little pressure gauge, located on the side, shot up and danced back and forth.

As he was turning around, he noticed a tall figure standing at the door, he thought maybe it was another employee, but he was the only male there, employee wise.  He reached for his flashlight that he carried on his belt, but when he shone the light at the door, there was no one there.  He hurried in to try to catch whoever was in the lobby, but there was no one there.  He went down and put the trash cart away, then went back to his office and looked at the security screen.

He found the one in the lobby, and rewound the footage to ten minutes before, and watched. He saw where his light was shining in through the door, but didn't see anyone standing in the door. Richard went to rub his brows and then something glitched on the screen.  Richard didn't catch it, but he rewound the footage again. He played it in slow motion and saw the glitch this time, he rewound and played it in slow motion again, this time stopping at the glitch. It was just a black spot, no definite outline, but Richard swore it was a tall man.

"Still gotta be my nerves," he said his heart racing a little, and then he took a sip of his coffee, "Gross! It's cold," he said to himself and turned the pot back on to reheat his coffee.

He spent the next hour or so looking at footage, checking to make sure there was no one around the building.  He watched over the nurse's station, then realized he left the curtains open. He got up and walked out of his office, then walked up to the dining room.

"Do you really have to shut them?" Cynthia asked.

"Yeah, it's on my list unfortunately," Richard said and walked up to the button next to one of the windows and pressed it.

The curtains started to draw together, with the main pulley being right next to the button. There was a cord with stopper to it that connected two motors, one at the base of the window and one at the top.  When the stopper hit the bottom motor pulley, it stopped, perfectly shutting the curtains.

Richard then took the scrubbing machine up to the lobby, even though it said mop, he didn't feel like messing with the mop bucket.  He repeated the process from the dining room, moved all the furniture to one side, scrubbed, then done the other side. Richard was proud of his work and went and drained the scrubbing machine. The water from the machine came out black, which confused Richard because the building was new and the floors didn't look that dirty. He done a second trash round, which wasn't much, a few bags and skipped the kitchen because no one was in there.

He dumped the trash and didn't encounter his phantom again.  By the time he put the cart away it was time to unlock the lobby doors.  There was one person waiting, even though it wasn't quite five-thirty yet.  It was a male CNA, with long, brown hair, pulled back and blue scrubs, he was broad shouldered, and looked as if he worked out, but wasn't defined by muscles just girth.  Richard opened the door.

"I hope I'm not late," the man mumbled as he brushed by Richard.

"They told me to unlock at five-thirty no sooner," Richard said but the man kept walking and went and got on the elevator without waiting for Richard.  The door was shutting when Richard walked up.  The man didn't even try to stop the doors from shutting, he just stared up at the light in the elevator.

Richard waited for the elevator, which seemed longer to come back up, then went into his office, once again his coffee was cold, even though he kept the pot on and refreshed his cup, it always seemed like whenever he left and came back, his coffee was cold. He turned off the coffee pot, then dumped what was left down the bathroom sink that was in his office. He went an opened the curtains and let the sun flood the main dining room and then turned on the lights. He then waited until six-thirty when there was knock on his door.  He opened it to see a man in his fifties, bald on top, with grey hair on the sides. He had thick, salt and pepper eyebrows, heavy set and his name badge read, "Mark".

"I'm Mark, you must be the night shift?"

"I am, I'm Richard."

"Anything happen last night that I need to know about?"

"No, it went smooth for the first night," Richard said, omitting the fact that he might have seen someone in the doorway.

"Well, I have to make my rounds, I guess I'm supposed to unlock the kitchen doors," he said and walked away.

Richard went back to his office, rechecked the camera, then clocked out. The heat was almost instant as he walked outside. His bike seat was wet with dew, so he wiped it down and rode home. He was happy with his first night of work.

His mom was still sleeping when he got home, so he couldn't share his enthusiasm of his first night of work.  He went and showered and thought about his night, thought about that ghastly figure in the doorway.  He crawled up under the sheets as the a/c kicked on, blowing cold air on his face.  He was soon, fast asleep and when Maria woke up, she made sure to keep quiet.

Maria made her way into the living room and in the corner she lit candles, knelt and prayed, thankful that her son returned home safely.

## Chapter Six: Tuesday

Richard woke up around six pm, to the sound of food being cooked.  He rubbed his eyes and got up quickly and raced to the kitchen.  There he found his Maria, cooking up a storm, "Hey momma!" he said as he walked over to her and gave her a peck on the cheek.

"I'm making you lunch for the night, but you have plate over there on the table," Maria pointed to plate of empanadas, refried beans and rice.

"Ohhh, thank you momma!" Richard smiled and raced to the table.

Maria stirred the pork she was making for pork tacos, she had been cooking it since after her prayer.  She tapped the wooden spoon off the ceramic pot that belonged to her mother, she hoped and prayed that one day she would be passing it down to Richard's wife.  She walked over to some dough she had made earlier and got her tortilla press, she made up about ten tortillas in about three minutes, she was a pro at it.  While Richard ate his breakfast so to speak she packed his lunch.

Richard helped clean up, until it was time for him to go.  The weather wasn't so sticky that night and he was able to breathe without problems from the humidity.  He rolled up to work, locked his bike and headed to the door.

Richard met Ron again at the door, Ron looked a little flustered he had a scowl on his face, "You okay Ron?"

"Yeah just a strange day, we had a resident fall, he said he was pushed, I reviewed the cameras in my office, but you have more in yours, I was wondering if you could review the ones in the west hall and see if you see anything.  He said he was coming out of the garden when it happened. Poor bastard cracked his head open, blood was everywhere. I got what I could, but could you run the extractor tonight down there to make sure?"

"Yeah, not a problem, I'll get clocked in and we can look together if you don't have anything else to do?"

"Yeah, that sounds good. I just wanna get out of here tonight with no more accidents," he said, he was visibly shaken, pale as if this slight mishap was the end of the world.

As they rode down in the elevator Ron was antsy, he kept wiping his hands on his pants and then wiping his forehead with the back of his hand. The elevator opened and Richard couldn't open his door fast enough, Ron basically pushed past him.

"What time did all this happen?" Richard asked, a little annoyed Ron just pushed his way in.

"Around six p.m. or so," Ron said and leaned over Richard a little.

Richard used a mouse for the computer screen that housed the west hall camera. He clicked on it, which brought up only that camera on the screen. He right clicked a box and it brought up different times and he clicked five-fifty-five p.m. and watched. A resident, walking with a walker was coming out of the garden. He looked like Mark, but older with large, square glasses that belonged to the 80's. He stopped for a brief second and looked behind him, then turned back around. When he turned back around, he left the floor and flew forwards. It didn't look like to Richard that he tripped, it did look like he was shoved, but nothing showed up on camera.

"Think he caught his foot on the threshold?" Richard asked.

"Did you see how he flew? He didn't even take a step, just flew," Ron said, irritation in his voice.

"I did, I'm just trying to think of something logical," Richard said, knowing there wasn't a logical explanation.

"I think this place still carries the ghosts from the past, I know we can't talk about it in front of the residents but, something is going on around here," Ron said, then there came a beep from Ron's pocket, "Well, time for me to go. Hope things stay calm for you tonight."

"Me too, try to relax once you get home," Richard said and followed Ron up to the door and locked it after he left.

Ron, sweating profusely turned around and watched as Richard went back down the elevator. Ron raced to his car, an older, grey Toyota and fumbled for his keys. He got in, slammed the door and took a deep breath. When he opened his eyes, he saw a figure in the back of his car. He screamed and reached for the gun under his seat, but when he turned to look back in the backseat it was empty.

"God dammit Ron, you're freaking yourself out," he said, then reached inside his glovebox. He pulled out a small bottle of cinnamon whiskey and drank about half it. The burn felt great and the cinnamon lit his lips on fire, "That should do ya until get home Ronnie-boy," Ron said to himself. He gathered his nerves for a few more minutes and then headed home.

Richard went back down to his office, made a pot of coffee, and looked at his list. He had to wax the dining room and lobby and try to extract the rest of blood stain. He went and made a round, checking all the doors, locking the ones he was supposed to and shut the curtains before he forgot to. Of course Michelle complained and Cynthia was nowhere in sight. Richard started folding the tables down and putting them in the closet. He was able to fit ten chairs on the dolly, so it didn't take him as long to put them up.

He then walked down to the room where the cleaning supplies was and observed the bloodstain on the carpet, it was mostly pooled up where the old door was at, which to Richard appeared more prominent. The rest of the carpet was fine except where it met the door. Richard made note to get to it while the floors were drying.

He went into the cleaning room and found the wax. He read it was quick drying wax, it would only take two hours to dry. He took the floor scrubber out and went into the dining room and scrubbed the floors. He then came back to the cleaning room and filled up his mop bucket to the recommended water to wax ratio and grabbed the shoe covers.

He slowly headed down to the dining room, passing Cynthia as he done so, "Hey, watch you up to?"

"I'm going wax the dining room and lobby, so please don't walk on them until I tell you to, please!"

"Not a problem!" Cynthia said and walked by Richard with a little bounce in her step.

Cynthia was a hard worker, she was raised that way. Her dad was strict but not abusive. She had worked her way up through school and was in college to be an LPN but The Gardens didn't hire student practical nurses, so she was stuck doing the dirty work.

Her next stop was Mr. Letrell, he was a retired Catholic Priest and by retired, he was tossed out of the Catholic church for exposing misconduct. He was usually nice, but here recently he had been a handful to deal with. Cynthia was hesitant to go in there.

Mr. Letrell was in his nineties, tall, but spent most of his day in a wheelchair. He could get up but would often lose balance and fall. The last couple nights he's felt a heavy presence. It's been messing with mentality, he knows it's been slipping, but recently it has slipped a lot.  He heard a knock on the door and then Cynthia came in.

Richard rolled the mop bucket up into the dining room and outlined the dining room with the wax, leaving the entry way open. He then went with a diagonal pattern first. He was halfway done with the dining room when had to stop and go get more.  He got the other side done, refilled, and headed to the lobby.  He was late doing the trash run, but he wanted to get the lobby done.

There was nowhere to put the furniture in the lobby, so he did what he didn't want to do and waxed around the furniture.  It only took one mop bucket to wax the lobby and took half the time to do the lobby than the dining room.  He went back down, filled up the mop bucket again and started in the second coat in the dining room. The floor looked good with one coat, but the second coat really made it shine, even when it wasn't dry yet.

He finished the dining room at three then went to go check the stain on the carpet, but once he got there it was gone.  He shook his head, knelt, and felt the carpet, it was dry, not a drop of blood in sight.  He sat there for a minute in disbelief. He then headed up to put the last coat of wax on the lobby.

He had his back towards the door, waxing the last corner when the doors jarred.  It caused Richard to jump and he looked back. There was no one at the doors that would cause the doors to try to slide open.  He looked outside to see if the wind was blowing and it wasn't. He went to turn around and someone jumped at him, he screamed out in terror. He brought his hands up to shield his face. He didn't get a good look at the person, but their face had a scruffy beard and a black ballcap hat. Richard slipped on the wax and fell flat on his back.   He hit hard, hard enough to knock the wind out of him.

"Uhhhh...shit!" he moaned out, as he laid there for second. The wax felt warm underneath his hands and was sticky as he lifted his hand up to look at the wax and expected to see wax, but instead he saw blood. He got up, struggling and slipping more there was blood everywhere. He looked in horror as the whole lobby was covered in blood, the couch, the desks, the floor. It was dripping from chandelier and running off the edges of the concierge counter "What the...." He struggled to breath, "what the hell?"

Richard looked in the mop bucket and it was filled with blood as well, everything he had waxed, was covered in blood. He freaked out and tried making his way to the elevator and slipped and fell again, blood covered his pant, shirt and hands. He finally made it to the elevator and when he looked back at the lobby, it was fine, not a drop of blood in sight. He checked his uniform and it was dry, not even wax was on it, like he didn't even fall. He grabbed his mop bucket in a hurry and headed downstairs, he calmed his breathing and wiped the sweat from his brow before the elevators opened. His heart was racing with confusion and fear.

He took his mop and bucket to the cleaning room and cleaned it out. He kept telling himself he was getting used to nightshift and was just over tired. He then went and done his trash run, except he went out the back-kitchen doors, avoiding the lobby, it was a longer trek around the building than expected. He dumped the trash, and looked around to make sure he didn't see anyone.

After the trash run, he was finally able to sit down. He made and poured him a cup of coffee and it tasted burnt.

"Damn it," he said as he turned the massager on the chair, because it felt like he had fallen, his body ached. He decided before it was time to put half the tables back, he would review the cameras to see they caught anything.

He clicked on the lobby camera and found the time from an hour before.  He watched as he waxed the floor and was at the corner, then it showed him putting the mop in the bucket and returning to the corner he had just waxed.  He just stood there, in the corner, swaying.  Then he suddenly turned around and was watching himself stare at the camera.  Then, he disappeared from the corner, Richard got a look of his confusion on his face as he clicked a different angle on the camera and he was standing by the elevator.

"What the fuck is going on," he said and took a sip of coffee, and once again it was ice cold. He spit it back in the cup and dumped it down the drain.  He then splashed water over his face and shook his head.

"It's just your imagination Richard," Richard said to himself, "All those years of watching all those haunted documentaries are catching up to you. You're just adjusting to night shift."

The whole time Richard was working, Cynthia was dealing with call lights and Mr. Latrell.  She walked in earlier and he was in the chair, staring at the garden.  He was silent and wouldn't talk to her, only when she asked if he need to use the bathroom, he responded, "No!, get out!" so she did.

Mrs. Malia down on east hall, was on her call light four times in half an hour after Cynthia got out of Mr. Latrell's room.  No matter how many times Cynthia moved the pillow, she couldn't get it right, so as requested by Mrs. Malia, Cynthia went and go someone who, "Knew what they were doing." Which she didn't go and get, she just left Mrs. Malia to adjust her own pillow.  She reported everything to Michelle, who wrote it down in the behavioral log and told Cynthia to take a break.

Michelle was having just as rough as a night as Cynthia.  Giving meds at nighttime was stupid in Michelle's eyes.  She hated waking the patients up to give them meds, with some, once they're up, they're up and of course Michelle gets the blame.  It's never the person who has smoked for years and has to take breathing medications or treatments, or the person who junked up their system and has to have shots for diabetes, it's always the nurses fault.  Michelle looked up from the desk and watched Richard get off the elevator.

Richard went back and sat out half the tables and chairs, he opened the curtains and unlocked the garden doors.  He went and reviewed the cameras once more, focusing on how he just stood in the corner without remembering standing there.  His phone beeped and he headed up to unlock the doors, he was met with the same rude guy, but Richard got his name this time, it was Doug.

"I hope I'm not late," Doug said, as he walked by and this time Richard fired back.

"Were you late yesterday?" Richard asked with some anger in his voice.

"No," Doug answered and looked surprised Richard said anything to him.

"Then shut up and quit bitching man," Richard said and flipped the door to open.  Doug stood there as Richard walked by, it was Richard who made it to the elevator this time and went down without waiting for the Doug, then went back into his office and shut the door.

His heart was racing, it was a strange night, he then remembered he needed to plug in the scrubbing machine.  He headed that way and as he walked by the nurse's station, he noticed Doug behind it, staring at him. He walked down and unlocked the room then plugged the machine in. He turned out the light and looked back, he didn't know why he looked back, but he did.  He noticed a light coming out from under the far wall.  It was moving, almost flame-like in nature.

Richard walked up to the wall, putting his hand on the scrubber handle as he done so, which caused it to move forwards.  It didn't hit hard, but it hit hard enough to crack the wall and the light got brighter.

"COOMMMMMEEE TOOO MEEE!" Richard heard a voice say beyond the wall.  Richard looked through the hole in the wall, he couldn't see much, but could see an old looking furnace of sorts, that had flames on the inside, "LLLEETTTT MMMMEEEEE OUUUUUTTTT!" the voice said.

Richard put his fingers in the crack and pulled at the drywall, it crumbled easily and the hole got bigger, he reached in again, "What are you doing man?" Richard heard Mark say, snapped out of his trance.

"Oh…I…uh..accidently knocked a hole in wall," Richard said.

"Well shit, as if I don't have enough to do around here, nurses left me note that said the lights were flickering this morning," Mark said, disgruntled.

"I'm sorry I didn't mean to do it," Richard apologized.

"Well I'll have it fixed, just don't let it happen again," Mark snapped and left.

Richard left the hole alone and went and clocked out then walked outside.  The humidity was back and couldn't say that he liked it.  He stopped off on the way home at a gas station to get something to drink. Then finished his ride home.  He took a hot shower hoping it would help him sleep.  He shut the blinds and cranked the ac and laid down, but no matter how hard he tried, he couldn't sleep. He tossed and turned right up until about thirty minutes before his alarm, then he fell asleep.

# Chapter Seven: Wednesday

Maria could hear her son tossing and turning, his moaning out then she swore she heard him say, "Jingling Jim," but he only said it once, if he said it.  She lit her candles and prayed once again for her son. She didn't like him working there, but she didn't want to ruin his hopes of becoming great at his job.

She quietly cooked for Richard, and then went to lay down. She heard his door and the fridge open and shut, then a few minutes later, the front door opened and shut.

Richard struggled to ride to work, his legs felt like jelly and his eyelids felt like they weighed a ton, but he made it and all he could think about was coffee.  Ron let him in and immediately started talking. Richard was in no mood for it.

"We had an issue with flickering lights in the garden, Mark tried to fix them but he said he called a professional because he doesn't believe it's the lights but the panel.  Other than that it's been okay, thanks for cleaning up the blood."

"Uh..yeah you're welcome," Richard said not wanting to admit that he didn't clean up the blood, that it just disappeared instead.

Richard went in his office, made a fresh pot of coffee, poured a cup and started drinking it before it had a chance to cool off.  He welcomed the hotness as it scorched his esophagus all the way down, "Maybe that'll wake me up."

He went into his bathroom and splashed some water on his face.  He went back and finished his cup of coffee, then got another one and started drinking it when he noticed lights flashing on one of the cameras.  He looked at it closer and it was one of the cameras in the garden, facing the rose garden.

The lights flickered and someone appeared on the camera, their back was facing the camera. They were tall, had a ballcap on, wore a one-piece, grey jumper.  Richard figured out at first it was one of the residents.   Then the person turned around and Richard couldn't look away.  The person had salt and pepper hair, and a small beard to match.  Their eyes are what got Richard, he couldn't stop looking into the cold grey eyes. The camera, without Richard's help zoomed in on the eyes.  Richard was lost in the eyes, they had a power over him where he couldn't look away.  Then he heard singing.

"Jingling Jim McCurdy, done the residents dirty!"

"Jingling Jim McCurdy, done the residents dirty!"

He heard it clear as day and then there came a knock on the door, which startled him. He looked at the door and when he looked back at the screen, it was back to being normal, the light wasn't flickering and there wasn't anybody there.  He opened the door and there stood Ron.

Ron looked at Richard, Richard's face was pale as could be, "You okay buddy? Look like you've seen a ghost," Ron asked.

"Yeah, just didn't sleep well," Richard said, "Maybe I'll wake up as the night goes on."

"Maybe so, I don't see how you night shifters do it."

"Hell, I don't even know how I do it," Richard laughed.

They walked together to the sliding doors, Richard flipped the switch on the door.

"You have a good night," Ron said and nodded.

"I will try my best," Richard said.

Richard locked the door behind Ron.  He turned back around and stopped a second as the memory of the lobby being filled with blood came back to him.  He shook his head and got on the elevator as quickly as he could.

The elevator started down, then halfway down, stopped abruptly, "What the hell?" Richard asked as he pressed the buttons on the elevator, none of them worked at all.  Then he heard the song he heard earlier, start playing over the intercom.  He opened the emergency box for the phone and picked it up, it was dead, it didn't ring out like it was supposed to. Panic started to overtake Richard, there was dark force at work and it's target was Richard.

"Jingling Jim McCurdy, done the residents dirty, Jingling Jim McCurdy, done the residents dirty....." the music continued with a slight jingling of keys in the background.

Richard hung up the phone and pressed the buttons again, and again nothing happened.  He then, out of anger and panic, decided to kick at the buttons.  The elevator jarred, then started to work, the music went back to the boring piano music it was before. The doors opened and Richard hurried out of the elevator.

He went straight to his office, grabbed a pink slip, wrote down the time and date, then wrote down what was wrong with the elevator.  He put the slip through the mailbox slit on the door for maintenance.  He then went up and talked to Michelle and Cynthia.

"The elevator is acting up, so just be careful if you have to use it tonight," he told them.

"I usually step out the back dock and smoke anyways, it's creepy back there though, I always feel like I'm being watched," Michelle said.

"I just figured I'd let you know, I just about got stuck on it. I'm going to get started, I have to scrub the dining room and lobby, then run the carpet cleaner up and down the hallways," Richard said.

He did his normal rounds, checking the doors, locking the garden doors, and shutting the curtains, then decided to put the table and chairs up instead of moving them to one side.  He scrubbed the dining room and put everything back, changed the water in the scrubber, then scrubbed the lobby.  He dumped and cleaned the scrubber and noticed the hole was fixed in the wall.  Richard stopped staring at it and made sure to keep his hand off the handle.

It was one, by the time he was done, and he decided to do the trash run.  He made his normal stop by the nurse's station and got their trash and headed towards the east hall trash room, then the kitchen. He went to the dock and grabbed the first trash can and it took all he had to pull the bag out.  He put the bag in the cart and turned to grab the other one, then jumped back and screamed, there was a head of an old man on the top of the trash.

"Shit ese! Shit!" he said and slowly turned back around to see if he was mistaken, he didn't want to look, but he did.  On top of the trash, wasn't the head of a human, but a head of cabbage. Richard shook his head, "You need to get some sleep ese," he said to himself, then grabbed the bag and tossed it in the cart then headed back towards the nurse's station.

"Hey! Have you seen Cynthia?" Michelle asked, standing in front of the station.

"No, I haven't, after I dump the trash, I will check and see if she's out around the building.  She might have let herself out front," Richard said.

What Michelle and Richard didn't know is Cynthia had been sweet-talking Ron into leaving her an Allen key for the garden doors and she had been sneaking out there since Tuesday. She learned Richard's schedule in the two nights and waited until he was busy and always made sure to lock them back.

Once Richard passed and Michelle went to the bathroom, Cynthia hurried down to the garden doors.  She inserted the Allen wrench into the bottom part of the push bar and pushed in.  She made sure to hold onto the doors so they didn't make a sound when she shut them.  She liked walking across the catwalk and sitting on one of the chairs overlooking the pond and listening to the waterfall.

That night she noticed the moonlight shining down on the rose garden. The roses seemed to sparkle under the moonlight and it really caught Cynthia's attention. She walked down and sat next to the roses.  She went to pluck one and a thorn pricked her finger.

"Ouch!" she said and put her finger in her mouth, but not before a drop of blood hit the soil.  Her blood acted like a catalyst for chaos.  As she went to get up and leave, a rotted corpse shot up from the rose bed, sending roses and soil everywhere.  Cynthia let out a scream as the corpse latched onto her throat and pulled her back into the rose bed.  There was a wet, crunching sound then a gurgle, then blood shot up from the hole that the corpse pulled Cynthia into.  It shot up about four feet then splattered all over the floor.

A second later, the blood got sucked back into the hole.  The soil was sucked back into place as well, then the roses all went back to where they were before.  There wasn't a trace of soil left, everything looked like it did before Cynthia came in.  All except the Allen wrench, which spun around on the floor for a second before stopping.

Mr. Latrell was in his room looking out the window when he say Cynthia walking by roses.  He had a bad feeling, but he couldn't reach the window to tap on it. Then the corpse shot out and grabbed Cynthia, "HELP! HELP! HELP!" he screamed.

Michelle heard the screams from down the hall and raced towards Mr. Latrell's room.  She struggled to find her keys, but finally did and unlocked the door and flipped on his light.  Mr. Latrell was having full on fit, screaming about Cynthia.

"IT GOT HER! IIIIIIITTTTT GOOOTTTT HEERRRR!" his face was all contorted in fear.

"What got who honey?"

"THE ROSES GOT CYNTHIA!"

Michelle looked out at the roses while trying to calm Mr. Latrell down.

"Mr..MR. LATRELL! CYNTHIA ISN'T EVEN OUT THERE!" Michelle yelled, she could only get hit so many times before she had enough.  She left Mr. Latrell in his fit and raced to her cart to get forty cc's of Ativan.  She raced back to his room and didn't even give Mr. Latrell a chance before sticking him.

Richard was making a round outside, looking for Cynthia when he heard a scream from inside. He was by the loading dock and rushed in.  He rushed up to the nurse's station and Michelle met him there with a worried look on her face.

"Did you hear that?" he asked.

"No, I was busy dealing with Mr. Latrell, what did you hear?" Michelle asked.

"I heard a scream out in the garden," Richard said.

"Mr. Latrell said he saw Cynthia in the garden," they looked at each other with worry on their faces and rushed to the doors.

Richard struggled to the get the doors unlocked, his Allen wrench didn't want to work. He pushed with his shoulders, and the doors finally opened.  Richard produced his flashlight, instead of turning on the lights and started looking for Cynthia.  Michelle and Richard raced all over of the garden looking and it was only when the

Allen wrench caught Richard's eye, that they stopped. He bent over to pick it up.

"What is it?" Michelle asked.

"It's the key to lock the doors, Ron must have dropped it out here."

"But where the hell is Cynthia?"

"I'll check the cameras and see," Richard said.

Richard put the Allen wrench in his pocket and headed back towards his office.  He made a fresh pot of coffee and waited until it was done before looking at the footage.  He sat down and set the cup down off to the side.  He then started to review the footage.  He watched as Michelle left the nurse's station and headed towards the bathroom located right behind the nurse's station.  He then watched as Cynthia looked up at the camera and left the nurse's station, keeping her eyes on the camera as she walked.  She then left the area and appeared on the camera facing the hallway leading to the elevator, she kept her eyes on the camera.  She then was seen on lobby camera, staring at it as she walked by, she reached up, unlocked the sliding doors and left.

Richard rushed up to the lobby to check the doors and they were flipped to where he flipped them but the lock was undone and he knew he locked it.  He thought Cynthia just flipped them open and then back just to get out.  It was weird to Richard that she just left without saying anything. Richard headed back down to tell Michelle the bad news. She was in the nurse's station and came out when she saw Richard.

"I looked at the camera's and looks like she just up and left. I'll see if I can send it to Sheila or James so they know. I thought she was a good worker," Richard said and scratched his head.

"She was, luckily there are only two residents that need help in the morning, so I should be able to take care of it," Michelle said, but Richard could see a visible look of concern on her face.

"I'm going to go see if I can email HR those videos, I'm not going to feel like staying over until they come in," Richard said, then left to his office.

He looked around through his desk to try to find a card with James's or Sheila's name on it, he found nothing. He started flipping through the schedule and luckily enough, on the last page, he found the email addresses of both of them. He chose to email Sheila instead of James, by right clicking on the video, then clicking "Send To" and typed in her email address. He hit send then went and got the carpet supplies.

He was all too familiar with the carpet cleaning process. He worked at a hospital once, on the floor crew. He used the process he learned there and applied it to the carpets at The Gardens. He found a backpack sprayer and filled it halfway up with the carpet cleaner, then filled the other half with water. He then grabbed the carpet bonnet that fit over the soft pad of a tile buffer and put it on the tile buffer. The tilted the buffer back on two tiny wheels and pulled it out into the hallway.

He put the sprayer on and pumped it up a few times and moistened the carpet with the solution. He done a ten-by-fifteen area, stopped, bonneted the area then went and onto the next area. He done that from the west hall all the way down east hall, then the hallway across from the nurse's station, to the elevator. He knew not to put too much solution down to soak the carpet, but just enough so the bonnet wouldn't stick and when he used the extractor to suck up the extra water, he done a few large sections before dumping the water.

It only took him an hour and a half to do the carpets, and another thirty minutes to suck up the water, but because of his technique there was hardly any water left.  He put everything away and looked at the time, it was just getting to be four.  He checked the closets for trash and the bags weren't even full so he left it.  He went and sat down in his office, reheated the coffee and drank a cup and turned on the massager.  He searched through the video feeds to see if anything happened while he was working and there was nothing.  He then decided to make a round before he fell asleep.

The elevator didn't act up anymore when Richard made his rounds.  He tried to stay moving because he was dead tired. He took time to admire how nice the carpets had come out when walking down to unlock the garden doors.  He went and opened the curtains and Michelle was there when he turned around.

"You know, despite how troublesome the night can be, I love watching the sun light up the garden."

"I probably would to, but I always have to go unlock the door for dipshit Doug then wait for Mark to show up," Richard said.

"I don't like that Doug, he's rather rude."

"He was to me too until I gave it back to him, then he quit talking to me, which I'm fine with," Richard laughed.

"I'll keep note of that," she said.

"Speaking of, I better go up and let him in before he has an aneurism," Richard said and headed up to the lobby. He didn't see Doug, but unlocked the door anyways and when he got back to the elevator, he turned and looked and saw Doug walking in the parking lot, towards the door.  Richard smirked and got on the elevator.  He went into his office, cleaned out the coffee pot and waited for the knock on the door.  It finally came and sounded a little lack luster, Richard started thinking the place was taking its toll on not just him

"Anything happen overnight?" Mark asked.

"Yeah, I left a slip about the elevator, it just stopped working, then started right back up and the phone quit working in there, I couldn't call out," Richard said.

"Well, crap, its rather new, so I don't think I can be hydraulics but I'll put a call in and hope they can get it figured out today," Mark said.

"And, not that it matters, but Cynthia walked out last night."

"Yep, you're right it doesn't matter," Mark said and went into the maintenance shop.

Richard clocked out, shut the door to his office and headed outside. A nice forecast had moved in, providing Richard with nice ride home.

He took his shower but was still having trouble sleeping. It was about halfway through the day, just when Richard had fallen asleep, that his phone started to ring. Richard's eye's shot open, "You have got to be kidding me," he said and reached for his phone, "Hello?"

"Hi Richard, it's Sheila, I don't mean to disturb you, but I was wondering about the videos you sent, what am I supposed to be seeing?" she asked.

"Um..uhh..." Richard rubbed his eyes, "It's of Cynthia walking out."

"I hate to tell you, but there's nothing on the videos, either of them," Sheila said.

"What? Are you serious?" Richard asked, stunned.

"Yes, there's nothing, is there a possibility you sent the wrong videos?"

"I might have, I'm sure I sent you the right ones, but I'll look tonight when I come in."

"Okay, as far as Cynthia goes, we have a replacement for her that'll start tonight, I know it's not your concern, but I thought I'd let you know."

"Thank you!"

"Try to rest, once again, sorry for disturbing you," Sheila said and hung up.

"Not an issue at all," Richard said as he put the phone on silent and tossed it back on the nightstand.  He wasn't able to get fully asleep for the rest of day.

# Chapter Eight: Thursday

Maria heard Richard's phone ring as she was in the middle of prayer.  She wanted to go check in on him, but something told her to let him be, so she did.  She noticed he didn't bring her lunch pail home so she didn't bother making him a lunch.

Richard got up early, and made a stop at a gas station on his way to work.  He grabbed a few energy drinks then carried on his way. He downed one of the energy before he even made it to work.

Ron wasn't there when he got to the door.  He got his keys out and unlocked the door from the outside and forcefully slid them open, then, shut and locked them.  He then heard the elevator and Ron came running off it, red in the face, sweat pouring down it. He was wiping at it wildly.

"I'm so sorry, there was a flood in w-thirty-three. I plunged and plunged and all this black sludge came up.  It finally went down," Ron said, still in a panic.

"It's all good, I got in and I won't be late.  You think I should look it at later or is it fine?" Richard asked.

"It's fine like I said, it went down. Mark is really mad at you for knocking a hole in the wall again," Ron said.

"What? I didn't knock a hole in the wall again, I made sure I didn't even get close with machine," Richard said confused.

"He left the drywall mud in the room and said you can fix it, well he was a little more expletive than that," Ron said.

"I guess I'm fixing a damned hole tonight," Richard said annoyed as they boarded the elevator.

Richard and Ron went their separate ways, Richard made coffee, but while it was making, drank another energy drink.  He then walked down to the cleaning room and looked where the hole was and sure enough, there was another hole in the wall.  It was three times the size of the hole he had made.  He shone his flashlight into the dark void of the hole. There wasn't a dancing flame like before and his light only appeared to go an inch or two into the darkness. He flipped the flashlight back off, stared at the bucket of drywall mud and putty knife, "What a dick!" Richard mumbled as he put his flashlight away.

He met Ron at the elevator and they rode up in silence.  He locked the sliding doors and double checked to make sure they were locked.  He then went back down and got him a cup of coffee.  He looked at the list and it stated he could wax if needed, and spot mop if needed.  He decided right then and there, it was going to be an easy night for him.

He made his first round, and as he was passing by the nurse's station to shut the curtains, Michelle spoke to him, "Hey Richard! This is Rachel, she's Cynthia's replacement."

Richard had forgotten to recheck the tapes, so he wrote it down in his pocket notepad for later, "I'm Richard, I'm the night security here."

"You mean glorified janitor," Racheal snarked.  Racheal was from a well-off family, with her slim body, blue eyes, and blond hair, she thought she was perfect and everyone else was inferior. She didn't even have to work.

"Well aren't you lovely," Richard said and walked away to shut the curtains.

"Maybe I want them open," Racheal said.

"Sugar, you ain't gonna win this one, they stay closed," Michelle said and laughed.

"We will see about that," Racheal sneered.

Richard walked over and shut the curtains, then walked back past the nurse's station, only to be glared at by Racheal.  He locked the garden doors, then headed out to check the dock doors.  He then went back to check out the dining room for areas that needed mopped and found a few spots.

He filled up a different mop bucket, with a blue cleaner for the floor and headed back to the dining when he caught the curtains opening and Racheal in standing next to the button.

"HEY!" he yelled and Racheal jumped, "I told you the curtains stay shut," Richard said hatefully and pressed the button to close the curtains. He gave Rachael one hell of a look.

"What's the big deal?" Racheal snapped, narrowed her eyes and stomped her foot.

"Listen, princess! The boss told me they stay shut at night and I open them in the morning and that's what happens.  I catch you messing with these curtains again, I will report you," Richard said.

"You're such a dick!" Racheal said and walked off.

"Thank you!" Richard said sarcastically and started walking around looking for spots to clean up.  He found several from spilled food, but nothing too concerning and mopped them up.  He then headed up to lobby and spot mopped it, afterwards took his mop bucket and cleaned it out.

He stopped and looked at the hole.  He took the drywall tape and top off the mud bucket, and dipped the putty knife in, getting a blade full of putty and went to the put some on the hole.  Just as he was about to cover up the top, smallest part of the hole, he heard a strange noise from within the hole and a fire-like light formed. The light caught Richard's attention and instead of fixing the hole he made it bigger, he started pulling larger chunks of drywall out. He made the hole big, big enough for him to crawl through.  He looked around with his flashlight and finally saw where the fire-like light was coming from.

Richard found himself in a room, that had long been forgotten. Tools hung from the ceiling and from what Richard could see, had layers of dust on them.  The light flickering came from a large, incinerator in the far-left corner of the room.  Richard could feel the heat coming from it. It was causing him to sweat.  Then, the flames died down, and room got dark, even with his flashlight still on.

Smoke rolled out from between the grates, then the handle popped up and fell to the side.  Richard knelt and opened the door and a big pillar of smoke hit him in the face. The smoke filled his nose and lungs, it was bitter smelling. He couldn't see at all and waved frantically at the smoke.  Then the smoke settled and he was able to see inside the incinerator.  He didn't see anything but a pile of ashes at first, a breeze came from out of nowhere and blew the ashes towards the back of the incinerator.

Richard watched as a skeletal foot appeared and as the ashes blew away from the foot, the tibia and fibula leg bones appeared, and then another foot and tibia and fibula, "Screw this!" Richard said to himself and went to turn around to leave. Something evil came out from the skeleton in the incinerator.  They latched into the wrists and calves of Richard.  He screamed out and tried to pull away, but he couldn't.  Then suddenly, he was yanked back into the incinerator and the door slammed shut.

Racheal realized Richard was taking a while doing whatever it was he was doing and Michelle was on break.  She walked over, done a double take to make sure Richard wasn't around.  She then ran up and pressed the button to open the curtains and watched with asmile on her face.  They started to open, then suddenly stopped.  The pulley went back and forth, the cord vibrated from the locked-up motor.

"Come on you piece of shit!" Racheal said and grabbed onto the cord with both hands and tried pulling it.  It didn't budge, so she gave it a hefty yank and it took off, catching her left hand in the pulley. The pulley acted like a surgical knife and sliced Racheal's hand clean off.  She screamed and grabbed onto it just below where it had gotten severed.  Blood squirted across the curtains and when Racheal fell to the floor, shot across the floor that Richard had just mopped.

The scream jarred Richard awake, he was outside the room and the hole was sealed up.  He was leaning up against the floor scrubber, "It was just a dream," he laughed to himself as another scream broke out.  He got up and ran out of the room and towards the screaming.  He rounded the corner of the nurse's station and Michelle was standing near the bloodied body of Racheal.

"CALL 9-1-1!" Michelle yelled.

Richard stared for a second, seeing the blood on the curtains, the wall and pulley system, "She tried to open the curtains, didn't she?"

"Does that matter? Call an ambulance!" Michelle snapped, applying pressure the Radial and Ulnar arteries, stopping what blood was left from leaving Racheal's body.

Richard got on the phone with 9-1-1, but felt the need to say something, "This wouldn't have happened if she left the curtains alone."

"No shit Sherlock!" Michelle said.

"Hello, I need to report an accident," Richard said and paused while the operator spoke, "Yeah, some princess had to have her way and got her hand chopped off," the operator spoke again, "Is she breathing?" Richard looked at Racheal, "She is for now, but probably won't be too much longer."

"RICHARD!" Michelle yelled, "WHAT IS WRONG WITH YOU?"

"Nothing, I'm fine...yes it's The Gardens, I'll meet the ambulance up front and bring them down," Richard said and hung up, "They're on their way, guess I'll be re-mopping tonight."

"Will you quit being such an ass and go get me some ice from the med room and put it in a bag, they're in there as well," Michelle demanded.

"I'll need your keys."

She tossed Richard her keys, "It's the one with the green cover," she said.

Richard went behind the nurse's station and could hear Mr. Latrell acting up again, and into the med-room where the ice machine was at.  Right next to the ice machine were one gallon sized, plastic bags.  Richard got the ice and put it in the bag, then held it up and looked at it, "Hope it fits," he laughed and spotted a bottle of peroxide and grabbed it.  He walked back out and tossed the bag of ice to Michelle, then heard the ambulance close by, so he headed up to the lobby.

He was met with flashing lights out front, he walked up to the doors, reached up, flipped the switch, and unlocked the doors.  There were two paramedics, one female, who was taller than Richard, had half her head shaved, and a bob hair cut on the other, she was from Puerto Rico and her partner, born and raised on the cornfields of Indiana, looked as if he picked up weights and never sat them down.

"Where's the victim?' the female asked as they passed through the double doors with a gurney.

"Victim of stupidity," Richard said, "She's down in the dining room, I'll take you, but all of us won't fit on the elevator. We can walk around and down to the dock, it'll take longer though."

"Or you could ride down with one of us and the other can ride down after, then we could all go together," the male paramedic said.

"Whatever you two want, you're the professionals," Richard said, and handed the other paramedic his badge, "you'll need this to get on." he said.

He led himself and the female with the gurney down and headed up the ramp. They were halfway up the ramp, when the male came out of the elevator and walked briskly up to them and handed Richard his name badge back. Richard led them right up to Michelle and Racheal who had regained consciousness, but was still fading in an out.

"So, what happened here?" the male asked.

"Someone messed with the curtains and they shouldn't have," Richard said.

"Richard!" Michelle said and stared at him.

"Well, you have a tourniquet on, the wound wrapped, she's awake, but her blood-pressure is low, which is expected with the blood loss. You done a great job!" The female said.

"Thank you!" Michelle said.

Mr. Latrell was getting louder and banging on the walls, "THE DEVIL IS COMING!" he yelled.

"I'm gonna have to sedate him again," Michelle said and got the Ativan, then disappeared into Mr. Latrell's room.

The two paramedics put a bloodied Racheal on the gurney. They loaded her up and Richard followed them up and locked the door behind them.  He went back down to the cleaning room, cleaned out a spray bottle and filled it up with peroxide.  He then filled up the mop bucket with hot water and found a scrub brush sitting on the shelf and he took some towels from clean linen room. He didn't know what he was doing, but something was telling him, he was going to get blood out.

He took everything back up to the dining room, then took the peroxide and heavily sprayed the parts of the curtains that were saturated.  The blood fizzed up and changed from a red to a faint pink.  He took the scrub brush and lightly scrubbed at the stains, he brought the brush in an upwards motion, to lift the stain. He then dampened a towel in the hot, mop water and pressed it to the treated blood stains, they lifted right off the curtains.  It took him almost two hours to get the whole curtain panel that was stained, clean.  He then took and mopped up the blood that was on the floor and when he was done, it looked as if nothing ever happened.

"It's kind of scary you know how to clean up blood like that," Michelle said, startling Richard as he admired his work.

"Yeah, it just kind of came to me," He smiled.

"Next time there's an emergency, don't be such a jerk!" Michelle snapped.

"I guess I'm just tired of the disrespect," the word "disrespect" just rolled off his tongue.

"I understand but that poor girl lost her hand."

"Which wouldn't have happened if she hadn't messed with the curtains.  I am sorry for my attitude, I haven't been sleeping well and it's catching up to me."

"I'll forgive you this time," Michelle joked, "Two CNAs in two days, this place isn't off to a good start. Looks like the past is catching up to this place."

"Yeah, doesn't help they never found Jim's body, probably haunting this place," Richard smiled.

"Jim?" Michelle asked.

"The guy that did all the killing and arson."

"I remember my parents talking about it, but didn't hear a name," Michelle said.

"I figured with as much as he's done, I'd be remembered," Richard said, the word "I" slipping out of his mouth.

"What? Why would you be remembered?" Michelle asked confused.

"What are you talking about?" Richard asked, even more confused.

"You said, "as much as he's done, I'd be remembered.""

"Told ya I'm tired," Richard rubbed his eyes, "I'm going to go dump this bloody water, then do my trash run," Richard said and walked away pushing the mop bucket with the mop. He went and dumped the water, he watched it as it went down the drain. He looked back over to where the hole was on the wall and couldn't believe it was perfect. It looked as if he had never ran into or crawled through it, if he had even crawled through it. That part was still concerning to him.

He grabbed the grey trash cart and went to west hall. Racheal had filled up both trash rooms in the short time she was there. Even in her absence she was haunting him. A lot of the bags looked as if they didn't need to be changed, they were barely half full. He had to take a load up before he even got to east hall. He threw everything in the compactor, slammed the door and pressed the button.  The trash compactor rumbled to life and a loud whine could be heard. Richard didn't wait until it was done compacting before he took the long way around and went into the kitchen through the dock doors, then got their trash.

He double checked to make sure there wasn't any body parts in the trash and loaded up the three, fifty-five-gallon bags and chucked them in the cart.  He then headed up east hall grabbed the trash there and then headed up back up the ramp to trash compactor.  He opened the door back up and when he did, thousands upon thousands of maggots came out the door, then out came heads, legs, and arms.

"Jesus Christ!" Richard said and stumbled backwards and fell. He scrambled to get to his feet, but when did there was nothing on the ground and the door on the compactor was open, "Get yourself together!" Richard said to himself and pushed himself up off the ground. He dusted the dirt off and finished throwing his bags away and headed in.

He went and checked his curtains and made sure they looked good, then went into his office and reviewed the tapes.  There wasn't one on the compactor so he couldn't look back and see if there were maggots and body parts, but he knew there wasn't, he knew he needed sleep.  He cracked open his third energy drink and drank it then, started up a pot of coffee.  An hour went by when he heard a knock on his door.  He opened it and there stood Michelle.

"Hey, I called and they sent yet another CNA to finish the night, her name is Dona, be nice to her, she's here and needing in," Michelle said.

"I will be, as long as she listens," Richard said and got up. He walked up to the lobby, his footsteps echoed in the empty lobby.  On the other side of the sliding doors was a short, older lady, about in her mid-fifties, long brown hair with blond tips and large, pink framed glasses.  She had a nervous smile on her face but didn't waste any time coming in when the doors opened.

"Hi, I'm Dona," she said, her voice shaky.

"Richard, I'm security."

"So, was you around when it happened? Michelle filled me in, but was you around?" Dona asked, giving the impression that she was nosey.

"No, I wasn't around, but I got the ice for her hand and cleaned up all the blood.  I will tell you the same thing I told her, the curtains are to stay shut until I open them, you understand that?" Richard said harshly.

"Yes...I...uh...understand," she said and Richard could tell he shook her nerves a little bit.

"I'll take you down and give you a quick tour, Michelle is busy. I'll show you the trash rooms, try not to fill them up to much," Richard said with a straight face.

"I will try not too."

"I'm just joking, I can tell you're nervous, just trying to lighten the mood. It'll give me something to do at four."

The elevator trip went in silence.  Richard showed Dona the trash rooms, and the massive dining room, and as soon as he was done, Michelle walked up and gave Donna a list of the residents and what, if anything needed to be done with them.  Dona started asking Michelle a thousand questions as Richard walked away she was already annoying him, and went to his office.

The rest of the night went in peace, his second trash run was light.  He then went back and propped his feet up. It came time to let Doug in so Richard got up and headed to the lobby.  He didn't see

Doug again and simply unlocked the doors and went back down.  He clicked on the camera to see if Doug showed up.  It showed Doug running through the lobby, he tripped and fell, then slid across the lobby floor.

"Damn man! That look like it hurt," Richard laughed as he rewound the footage and watched it again, then laughed even more the second time around.  A few seconds later he heard the elevator open and the shuffle of feet.

He watched the footage a few more times, then came a knock on the door. He opened it and it was Mark, who looked like he had just woken up, "Did you fix your damned hole?"

"Yes, I did, you can't even tell I put a hole there," Richard gloated.

"Anything new?"

"Night shift CNA cut her hand off on the curtain motor, sprayed blood all over curtains, but I think I got them cleaned," Richard said, gloating again.

"Well, that doesn't happen every day," Mark said.

"Let's hope it doesn't happen again," Richard said.

"Let's hope not, you have a good day," Mark said, "I have list of lights out in the garden again, they keep blowing for some reason."

Richard cleaned up his office, tossed his cans, cleaned out of the coffee pot, then it was time to leave. There was cloud cover again, so the ride home wasn't too bad.  He made it home, skipped his shower, fell face first on his bed and just laid there, waiting to fall asleep, his energy drinks seemed to kick in all at once, right as he was laying down.

## **<u>Chapter Nine: Friday</u>**

Richard hardly slept at all again, his mom was even gone half the day, he was glad it was Friday and he was off Saturday and Sunday. He managed to get an hour of sleep before his alarm, but had a horrible nightmare.

He was back in the incinerator room and it was on, flames danced in eyes, a slight jingle of keys echoed in the room, then laughter. Flames shot out of the grates, causing Richard to jump back. The door flung open and the flames shot out even more, Richard shielded his eyes and the flames disappeared. When he brought his arm down, there stood a man he had only seen slightly before. He was tall, salt and pepper hair and beard, dark circles under his eyes and the nastiest teeth that Richard had ever seen.

"Who are you?" Richard asked.

"You know who I am, I am you and you are me. Say my name Richard, you know who I am, say it!" the man taunted.

"You're….you're…Jingling Jim McCurdy," Richard stuttered.

"Mmmmmm," he growled, "I used to hate that name, now I welcome it."

Richard didn't have a chance to respond when Jingling Jim leapt and screamed. Richard shot up in the bed and screamed out, sweat pouring his down face. His mom was still out, so there was no one there to come check on him. He sat up on the edge of the bed and wiped the sweat from his brow. He then got up, took a shower that he skipped earlier, and headed out to work.

He made a pit stop at the gas station.  Even the cashier noticed he was looking a little rough, "You doing okay man, you look hella tired?" the American born Indian said to Richard.

"Yeah, been a rough week at work, people walking out, hands getting cut off, messed up."

"Oh my goodness!" was the only response the cashier had for Richard, who paid and headed back towards work.

Ron was waiting on him this time, "Hey! How's it going?" he asked.

"Still not sleeping the best, but I'll get there. I should be gold after this weekend," Richard said, saying he'd be gold was something he's never said before.

"Yeah, been looking forward to the weekend since Monday," Ron joked.

"Yeah same."

They walked to the elevator and when they got in Ron asked, "So did the night CNA really chop of her hand?"

"Clean off at the wrist, which wouldn't have happened if she would have left the curtains alone."

"All the nurses do on my shift is play with them, but they didn't even touch them tonight," Ron laughed.

"Good, I've already told Dona not to mess with them," Richard said and they stepped out of the elevator.

"Dona hasn't shut up since she's clocked, in, you can hear her from one end of the building to the other," Ron said and seemed irritated, "See ya in a bit!" Ron said and went into his office.

Richard done his normal, making some coffee, reviewing the cameras.  He downed an energy drink again before a cup of coffee.

Then, for some odd reason he took his keys and let them hang on the outside of pocket, when he moved, they jingled, "That's what I'm talking about."  He then looked at the list, he was to scrub and buff the dining room and lobby. Then came the knock on the door, that let him know Ron was ready to go home.

"Ready to leave weasel?" Richard said without thinking.

"I'm sorry what?" Ron asked offended.

"You ready to go?" Richard chuckled.

"Yeah, but you called me a weasel."

"And?"

"I'm not a weasel, so don't call me that, okay?"

"Geeze! Sorrrrray!" Richard said and they boarded the elevator.  They rode up in silence, but Richard broke the silence as he let Ron out, "Hey! I'm sorry! You have a good weekend."

"It's good man, hope all goes well for you tonight and you have a good weekend too!" Ron smiled and walked away.

Richard put his keys jingled as he walked. He had a grin on his face as he boarded the elevator.  He walked down the hall and his keys got the attention of Michelle and Dona, they stared at him for a second, but stopped when he stopped and stared back.  Michelle looked away and rolled her eyes as she done so.

He walked into the dining room and put the tables and chairs up, shut the blinds, then stopped to admire his work on the curtains "Hey Michelle!"

"What?"

"You can't even tell Racheal lost a hand, not a drop of blood in sight," Richard boasted.

"Too soon Richard," Michelle said and went behind the nurse's desk where Richard would have to press a button to talk to her.

Richard was still admiring his work when he heard a voice off to the side, he didn't catch what was said but when looked there was man who was still tall for even being in a wheelchair. He was staring dead at Richard. He said what he said a second before again, "Devil!"

"Mr. Latrell, I'm in no mood for your shit tonight, go back to your room!"

"DEVIL!" Mr. Latrell pointed at Richard and started to roll himself towards Richard. Mr. Latrell started praying, he was praying in Latin. The words he spoke, Richard didn't understand, but they hurt him.

Richard fell to one knee, his heart tensed up, his eyes went blood red as he choked up. Mr. Latrell rolled right up to him, then stood up. In the background Michelle was rushing to get the shot. Mr. Latrell produced a cane and brought it up above his head, his eyes narrowed and anger rose in him as he screamed out. Richard tensed up, expecting to be cracked in the head. Richard heard a thump, but never felt a blow come to him. The pain in his chest went away, he opened his eyes and looked up. Mr. Latrell was slumped over in his chair. Michelle was standing there with a needle and a smile on her face.

"Told you Mr. Latrell, I ain't in no mood. You okay honey?"

"Yeah I thought for sure he was going to crack me," Richard said and stood up, dusting off his knees, "Well enough excitement for one night, I need to get to work. Thanks for the save," Richard said.

"Anytime!" Michelle said and wheeled Mr. Latrell back to his room. He was deadweight and it took all she had to get him into bed. She noticed he was.

Afterwards Richard went down and loaded up the scrubber with the cleaning solution and walked back down to the dining room. On the way Dona came out of a room and rambling on something about a T.V. remote, but Richard ignored her and kept on walking. He turned into the dining room and started scrubbing, he made an outline and when he started coming around to the entrance, Dona stepped out in front of him.  He swerved the machine to keep from hitting her and let go of the handle, which stopped the waterflow.

"WHAT THE HELL IS WRONG WITH YOU?" Richard yelled.

Dona looked shocked as if she done nothing wrong, "I tried telling you about a remote and you walked on by."

"So!"

"Well, go fix it," Dona demanded.

"First of all, you're not my boss, you don't sign my paychecks or make my schedule, so you don't tell me what to do. Secondly, remotes aren't a security thing." Richard snapped.

"Well he's going to keep harassing us until you do," Dona said.

"You know what, I'll look at it, but not because I want to but because your voice is annoying and I don't want to hear you talk anymore," Richard grabbed back onto the handle of scrubbing machine, "I have to finish the dining room and lobby, now get off my floor!" he snapped and started the machine back up.  He made a couple of trips before Dona left the floor.

He went to the lobby after putting all the tables back and moved the furniture there and started scrubbing.  He took twice as long to scrub it in hopes that whoever wanted their remote fixed, was bothering the hell out of Dona.  He moved all the furniture back and headed down the elevator with the scrubber.

He was met by Dona, "What is taking you so long to look at that remote? He's been harassing us the whole time you've been gone."

"My actual job, go away!" Richard said as he walked by Dona.

"It's Mr. Paterson if you're wondering, in room west-thirty-five."

"I wasn't, but thank you!" Richard said and smiled knowing he was getting on her last nerve. He drained the scrubber and rinsed it out, then on his way back, stopped off at west-thirty-five.

He took his west, master key out and stuck it in the slot, then knocked on the door, "Mr. Paterson, it's security."

"Come on in, it took you long enough!" Mr. Paterson said, his voice cracked with age, and slight northern accent.

Richard opened the door and went in, Mr. Paterson, was sitting in a brown recliner, in front of a large, sixty-five-inch T.V., he was a rather large man, from what Richard could see. His hair was too dark for a man his age and it looked like a toupee. The recliner was faced away from the door, but enough where Mr. Paterson could see who came in. His face was crinkled in angst and his big eyes, narrowed.

"I can't get this damn T.V. to work, keeps saying "No Source Detected," I don't know what in the hell that means. That last lady wasn't smart enough to figure it out, I hope you're not as dumb," Mr. Paterson griped.

"I'll see what I can do," Richard said and took the remote to study it. It had a source button so he pressed that and an input screen came up so he scrolled down to an HDMI and waited a second, then a picture popped up, "There you go," Richard handed him the remote back.

"Well, aren't you just a smarty-pants," Mr. Patterson yanked the remote away from Richard, "Next be quicker about it, I thought I was going to die waiting."

Richard shut his eyes for a second time and when he opened them, they were a stone-cold grey. He slowly moved back and behind Mr. Paterson, who thought Richard was leaving. Richard snagged pillow out from behind Mr. Paterson's head and put it over his face. He leaned back pushing the pillow into Mr. Paterson's face before he could scream.

Mr. Paterson tried to fight, he grabbed for the pillow wildly, but Richard was too strong for him. He pulled at Richard's arms, but he couldn't budge them. Richard leaned back even more and pulled the pillow against Mr. Patterson's face even more. Mr. Paterson's legs were kicking hard at first then slowed. His tight grip on Richard's arms started to lighten, then they fell to the side as his legs quit moving. Mr. Paterson was dead.

Richard put the pillow back under Mr. Patterson's head. His eyes were still open, so Richard used two-fingers on his right hand, in the shape of V to shut them, "Now you won't die waiting, because you're already dead!"

Richard shut the door and locked it, he shut his eyes again and when he opened them, they were back to being brown. His memory was of him walking out of the room, not killing Mr. Patterson. He looked at his watch and it was close enough to the time to do a trash run. So, he walked two rooms down and got the trash cart, hit the west trash room, then headed down to the east hall. Trash was light for Friday night, even the kitchen trash was light, he was able to get it all done in one load. He then headed to the trash compactor.

He took in the heavy air, it was thick with moisture and Richard didn't like it. He looked at the stars that littered the sky and the halfmoon. He patted his keys headed into the lobby and back down to put the trash cart away. He was heading back up when he Dona stopped him.

"What do you want now?" Richard asked and rolled his eyes.

"The funeral home will be here at four-thirty, Mr. Paterson passed away and you need to let them in," she said and put her hand on her hips.

"Glad I got his T.V. fixed so he could have spent his last hours watching it," Richard said, "Oh, and quit telling me what to do, you....are...not...my....boss!"

Richard turned around and walked away, he went into his office, drank the other energy drink, and heated up some coffee and drank a few cups of that.  He rewound some footage of right before he came out of Mr. Patterson's room.  He watched himself come out, then rewound it and watched it again, the second time he came out, it wasn't him. The person had their face away from the camera as the they locked the door.  The camera glitched and the figure of the man, wasn't Richard, the figure was Jingling Jim.  He brought his right hand up and it was covered in blood and waved at the camera by wiggling his fingers.  Richard rubbed his eyes and Jingling Jim was gone and there was only the image of an empty hallway.

Four-twenty rolled around and Richard got up, to head up to the lobby and before he could even put his handle on the doorknob, there was a knock. Richard whipped the door and there stood, none other than Dona, Richard brushed right by her and walked up to the elevator. Dona was talking, but Richard was in a whole other world. He got on the elevator and Dona was walking back up the ramp, Richard lifted his middle and flipped her off as the doors shut.

He noticed a minivan out front instead of a hearse, he found it kind of odd. He flipped the switch and unlocked the door open. There stood a woman, with short hair, buzzed on the sides and spikey on top.  She wore black-framed glasses, a black suit and tie.  The only way Richard knew it was woman was because of her breasts, which she made sure Richard could see by pushing her chest out.

"I'm here to pick up a body," she said and smiled.

"What the hell is up with the minivan?" Richard asked.

"We're using those now to be more discrete," she said and Richard noticed her nametag.

"Well Ramona, the minivan takes the spooky factor away, and I can't say I like it. Follow me, I'll take you down and have the nurse take you the rest of the way."

"It's not a bloody mess is it?" she asked.

"Nope, he died in his recliner from too much excitement on the television," Richard smirked.

Richard led Ramona down the elevator and into the hallway leading up to the nurse's station.  Michelle was waiting at the cross section and took over guiding Ramona to Mr. Paterson.  Richard realized he didn't do a second trash run, so after checking the closets, they were practically empty, decided he didn't need to do another one.  Then caught Ramona as she was leaving and followed her back up and let her out.

"You have a good morning," she said.

"I'm having a better one than him," Richard nodded and shut the doors before Romana could respond. He locked it, nodded at Ramona, who was still staring in disbelief of what she had just heard.

He went to his office and watched as Mr. Patterson was loaded into the back of the minivan and they drove away.  Richard wiggled his fingers in a wave like manner and smiled.  He downed another energy drink, they didn't appear to be working but he kept hoping they would.

It was soon time to let dayshift in. He went up and unlocked the door again, this time there was a young female, with black hair, blue eyes, and full-sleeved tattoo of the solar system up her arm. She walked by and smiled, "I'm Lisa!"

"I'm Richard, I was expecting Doug but forgot this was Saturday morning. Nice to meet you!"

She nodded and walked by and that's when Richard caught her scent, she was wearing a perfume that smelled like pineapples. She had a little bounce to her walk and Richard watched her walk all the way to the elevator then turned his head before he was seen. He went back down and cleaned up his office for the day.  It was soon time for Richard to clock out.  He biked home and had breakfast waiting for him when he got there and his momma was there with a smile.

# Chapter Ten: Saturday

Richard was excited to see the breakfast on the table.  There were chorizo sausage patties, eggs, thick cut bacon and some honey biscuits, milk, orange juice, and coffee.  Richard took a biscuit, sausage and bacon and let the sweet and heat dance on his tongue. He stopped and grabbed the salt, which his mom narrowed her eyes at, then dumped a bunch on the eggs, then grabbed the pepper and done the same.  He took a big bite and let the egg yolks run down his chin.  His mom reached over and smacked the back of his head.

"I made you this breakfast, you can at least eat it with respect," she said.

"Sorry momma! It's been a rough week and this is really good," Richard said and slowed down on eating.

"You're welcome!" she said and got up to go into the front room.  The minute she left, Richard shoveled the food in his mouth again, he chugged the milk and orange juice, then threw all the dishes in the sink instead of washing them, like he usually had done.  He avoided the shower and went and laid down in his room.  He heard his momma cussing in Spanish as she done the dishes later.  He smiled before dozing off.

He got to dreaming and he was dreaming he was at work.  He was doing a trash run and opened up the west hall trash room and there was nothing but severed heads, the resident's heads, Sheila's and James's head, Michelle's and Donna's as well. The closet was full of heads and the scary part was, Richard was okay with picking them up.  He was watching through his eyes, but he had no control over what he was doing.  One after another he picked up the heads, then when he picked up Sheila's, he kissed it for some reason, then tossed it in the cart.

The cart was full of heads, so he headed out to the compactor.  The walls started dripping blood as he walked down it towards the elevator.  He made his way out to the compactor and it had taken on different shape, with two, twenty-four-inch round, exhaust pipes out the side and up towards the sky, which was odd because it was a compactor.  Richard walked up and opened the door and there were flames inside.  He tossed in a head in and the flames on the inside reared up.  He continued to toss more and more heads in until the cart was empty.  He shut the door and pressed the button and flames shot out of the exhaust pipes, and mushroom clouded into the sky.  As the compactor/incinerator whined, the flames shot up higher into the sky.  The whole thing shook and rattled as it operated.

Richard headed back down and opened east hall trash room.  It was full of arms and legs.  He looked over and there stood Jingling Jim, he smiled and grabbed onto two arms and started juggling them, spraying blood all over Richard's face, but Richard smiled.  Circus music started playing, then Jingling Jim suddenly appeared on a unicycle and continued to juggle.

"Enjoy the show, kiddo, it gets better from here," Jingling Jim said and spun around on the unicycle.

"Why is this happening to me?" Richard asked.

"I owe you one, sins of the father Richard, sins of the of the father," Jingling Jim said and stopped juggling, the arms made a wet, slopping noise as they hit the floor.

"What's my father have to do with this?" Richard asked confused.

"More than you know," Jingling Jim said, then suddenly, Jingling Jim's head started to grow three times its size.  He let out a growl as his mouth opened wide, revealing rows and rows of sharp, jagged teeth.

Richard took off running, and Jingling Jim gave chase on the unicycle.  Richard looked ahead of him and the end of the hallway got further and further away, he looked back and Jingling Jim was gaining on him.  Richard couldn't move fast enough, a darkness surrounded him and the teeth appeared above his head, then darkness as he heard crunching. Richard woke up screaming, covered in sweat.

His light came on and Maria was standing there, "Are you okay?" she walked over to his bed, clutching her rosaries.

"Yeah, just another nightmare, but it was a weird one, someone mentioned dad," Richard said and the life drained out of his mom's face.

"What..what do you mean?"

"Someone in my dream mentioned dad, momma, that's what I mean.  He was tall, slender man, dark circles around his eyes, hardly any teeth, well, at first," Richard said, describing Jim from the first time they met and not from the dream he just had. He purposely didn't mention Jingling Jim's name, to see if his mom would confess anything.

Maria took a deep breath and even though she still had a worried look on her face, she said, "I think you're thinking too much about your father."

"I haven't really," Richard said and wiped some sweat from his brow.  Maria left and he looked at the time, it was only eleven-forty-five a.m., he had only been asleep a few hours, but was wide awake.

He got up and headed to the kitchen, there was new set of dishes in the sink.  He decided to wash them, to make up for not doing them the night before.  While he was washing the dishes, he did start thinking about his father.  He wondered what Jingling Jim was talking about or maybe he was just delusional from lack of sleep. He wanted answers and the library didn't close until three p.m., so he was going to take a trip after doing dishes.

He left without saying anything and biked to the public library a few miles away.  The heat was horrible that day.  He had sweat in places he shouldn't, but he wanted to get to the library. He knew they'd have some articles even though the ones he was shown, they never mentioned any names of those who shoved Jingling Jim in the incinerator.

He stopped to grab a drink at another gas station right next to the library.  He was only fifty yards away, but he needed the refresher as he felt lightheaded from the heat.  He slurped down his drink, tossed it next to the trash bin and biked the fifty yards.

The library was a two-story building with white siding and black shutters. There were large, concrete steps on the northern and western parts of the building. It looked like a large home instead of a library, with slight modifications for easy access.  He parked his bike in the bike rack and went inside.  There was a desk right in the middle of the library where the Librarian sat.  He was an older man, slender with sunken in face, thin, black glasses and bald. He was wearing a pink, long-sleeved shirt, with plaid pink and green, vest.

"How can I help you?" he asked smiling.

"I'm wanting to look up stuff on The Gardens, older stuff, not newer stuff."

"Oh! The fire of 87', that was horrible.  We have a whole folder in the back, every article ever written on it, including obituaries. I can take you back there if you like and show you?" the Librarian offered his help.

"Sure that would be great!" Richard said followed the Librarian to a corner of the library.  It had an old magnifier that looked like a computer screen.

"This will help you see the articles, they're kind of old, but all you do is flip this switch," he flipped a switch on the side of the screen and a light came on inside the cavity of the screen, then you set what you want to look on here," he pointed to black, metal table housed underneath the screen, "and it'll bring it right up," he smiled.

"Thanks," Richard said and stared at the old machine.

"And here's the folder," the librarian said and handed Richard a faded, yellow folder that was about three-inches thick, there was a visible layer of dust on it.  He wiped off the dust with his hand, then wiped his hand on his pants.

Richard said thanks again and took the folder and opened it. The first ten articles looked familiar, it's ones he's read before.  Then came an article he hadn't seen before, it was the obituaries.  He scanned through and wasn't for sure what he was looking for, then Jim McCurdy popped up and he stopped and read it. It stated he had a wife and one son, named Johnathan.  Richard took out his phone and made a memo of the name.  He scrolled through a couple more articles then came another one he hadn't seen.  It was titled, "Hero of The Gardens goes insane!"  He proceeded to read then stopped when his dad's name appeared, Rico Ruiz.  He knew nothing of his dad being a hero or involved in The Gardens at all.

He continued to read how it was his dad who had gotten down into The Gardens after the elevator was broken.  His dad was the first on the scene to see all the dead bodies and blood trails that were left by Jingling Jim and finally, it was his dad who stopped Jim and managed to escape before the building burnt down.  It didn't say how his dad stopped Jim, but Richard did find him in an incinerator, or he dreamed he did.

Richard knew his dad went insane, but never knew why. He also knew where the asylum was at that his dad lived in.  He was never allowed to go visit his dad though, Maria would go, but never would take Richard. He knew he had to go talk to his father, but he doubted his father would even recognize him.  Visiting days were Sunday at the asylum and he was going to bother his mom to take him or drive himself.  He put all the articles back and took the folder back up the Librarian.  He thanked him and headed back home.

The ride home was a long one, Richard was deep in thought on why his momma kept it from him.  Why did she lie about her dad all these years.  He didn't even put his bike up right, he simply got off it, mid-pedal and let crash into the ground.

Maria was waiting for him when he whipped the door open, "Where have you been? I've been trying to call you."

Richard cut to the chase, "I want to go see dad," he was expecting a battle from his mom, but she put her head down and sighed, as if admitting defeat before the battle even started.

"I knew this day would come," her eyes got teary, "I will take you tomorrow, during visitation.  I warn you, he's been in a vegetative state for a long time because of his meds."

"I just need to see him," Richard said.

"Tomorrow son, I promise," Maria said, "I need to lay down, I get tired easily at my old age." She was grasping her rosaries and shook her head as she walked way and went into her room.  She went to shut the door and stopped and stared at Richard.  She wasn't recognizing her son anymore.

Richard was left alone, but couldn't fall back to sleep so, once it got dark, he biked out to The Gardens to see if he could catch a glimpse of the nightshift guy on the weekends.  To his surprise as he watched and waited for a trash run, it was nightshift girl.  She was taller than him and wore a hat with her ponytail through the back. He kept his distance so she couldn't see him, but he didn't feel weird creeping on her either.

Richard left and went home, he stayed up the rest of the night watching T.V. in his room, then dozed off around eight a.m..

# Chapter Eleven: The Asylum

Even though Richard went to bed early in the morning, he was up by twelve, took a shower and got dressed. He wore a blue and white striped shirt, with blue jeans. His nerves were shot from the thought of seeing his dad after so many years, so he made some coffee to calm his nerves, it always helped him.

"I don't see how coffee helps calm your nerves," Maria said and walked up beside Richard, "I get jittery when I drink it, but it's always helped you, just like your papi." Maria was wearing a dress with yellow sunflowers on it and carried a little white purse, "Are you ready to go? Visiting hours are at two."

"Yeah, momma I'm ready," Richard said and sat his blue, coffee cup down.

They left and headed up a place just north of Yertzville, about a twenty-minute drive. The asylum or LaRuse Del Carto was the name on the front of building was massive. It was a four-story brick building, with fifty-five-degree pitched, green and metal roof. There were two towers, one on each end of the building that towered over the rest of the building, it gave Richard the creeps. Ivy ravished the brick from top to bottom, in all directions, some even covered the windows.

There was a big, parking lot on the side of the building, and for it to be visiting day, was rather empty. Maria parked the nineteen-ninety-nine Buick Regal, gold in color, with the back, quarter-panel dented in from a car wreck. They stepped out and stopped to stare at the building once more. The parking lot, even though it looked as if it were covered in asphalt, had a gravel feeling to Richard as he walked on it. It even sounded like they were walking on gravel. The parking lot was in need of massive repair.

There were concrete steps leading up to the main door, that were easily fifty yards long. There were about seventy-five of them and Richard helped his mom up each one.  They had to stop half way up, so Maria could rest a few minutes before continuing up the steps.

The doorway was a large, metal, arched doorway with a handle on the outside used to pull it open.  Once inside there was a large, walk-thru metal detector.  Richard and Maria had to set their personal belongings on a small conveyor belt as they walked through.  The police officer there, a stocky built, buzzed cut man with a mustache, round face and light blue eyes, checked their belongings through a small X-ray machine. Then the officer passed everything off onto another small, conveyor belt that brought their belongings to them on the other side of metal detector.

Beyond that was a towering, domed entrance way, with white, marble flooring and skylights in the ceiling.  Richard's and Maria's footsteps sounded heavy on the floor as they walked. Everything echoed and was extremely loud. They walked down a hallway that was brick as well, but painted a peach color, and when they turned the corner, an eerie silence fell over them and no noise could be heard from the entrance way.

They went through a set of pea-green double doors, then was met by a security guard, who was taller than the officer, but just as stocky.  He held a clipboard, and he acted like he knew Maria.

"Welcome back Maria, it's been a few weeks," he stopped and looked at Richard, "Is this your son?"

"Yes, I finally brought him with me after all these years."

"Nice to meet you! I've been seeing your mom here on Sundays for quite some time," the guard said stuck out his hand.

"Nice to meet you," Richard said and shook it.

"You know where to go from here, they'll bring him up shortly," the guard said and opened a single white door for Richard and Maria to step through.

There was another long hallway, that had windows on the top three feet on the wall, of the left part of the hallway, with pastel blue, cinder blocks with a lot of chipped paint.  The magnificent flooring stopped at the single door and was replaced with tile that had long been neglected.  It was blue, white, and grey speckled, with broken corners and some spots that looked like blood stains.

They rounded a corner and the hall split in two, the other hallway was ninety degrees to the other hall that Richard and Maria stayed on.  There was another set of double doors that they opened and led to a room, that appeared to be the visiting room, it was small, had about seven tables with chairs and no one was in there.  Richard and Maria sat down at a table and waited.

A few minutes later, a set of doors opened on the opposite wall of the double doors they used to enter.  A medium sized, beige skinned man, with curly, light brown hair walked in, pushing a man in a wheelchair.  The man had thick, grey hair. His head hung slightly to the right and his bottom lip drooped to the right was well.  His right eye was drawn down and his face was littered with stubble.  A good amount of drool hung from his lip and dripped on his blue sweatsuit. His arms hung inside the arms of the wheelchair and there was no facial expression from him when he saw Maria or Richard, but he wouldn't know who Richard was.

"Here you go Mrs. Ruiz," the nurse said, locked the wheelchair and walked away.

"Richard…this is your father, Rico. Rico this is Richard," Maria said.

"Hey, pops.." is all Richard could get out before breaking down in tears at the sight of his father.  Rico took a breath and even though he had no facial expressions, a tear formed in his left eye and fell down his cheek.

"Both you stop crying," Maria said as her eyes began to get teary, she reached over and wiped tear off Rico's face, "That's the most emotion I've gotten from him in a long time."

"Has he always been like this since he's been in here?" Richard asked and composed himself.

"This happened about a year after he got committed in here. He was complaining of nightmares, but the doctors thought it was his psychosis acting up. Then one day they found him in his bed, with a stroke. So I get worried when you have nightmares, I believe whatever he was having nightmares about, is what caused his stroke."

Richard was sure he knew what his dad was having nightmares about, but he didn't say anything to his momma about it. He was getting ready to say something when Maria said, "I have to use the restroom, stay here and maybe talk to him, he will enjoy it."

Maria got up and left and Richard was left with his dad. He scooted closer to his dad, "I know you don't remember me much, but I bet you remember Jingling Jim McCurdy," he whispered the name, then his eyes went from brown to grey.

Rico's eye grew wide and he made a strange, raspy, breathing sound, his hands and feet twitched, then he yelled out in some kind of gurgle, scream mixture. It made Richard move back and the nurse from earlier came running in.

"Shjinglin Shjim, shjingling shjim!" Rico started yelling in an attempt to say Jingling Jim. Rico shot back in his chair and yelled out the name, spittle flew through the air. He soiled himself, it then started dripping down and out his wheelchair.

"What's going on?" the nurse asked, concerned,

"I don't know, he just freaked out!" Richard said and sat back, his eyes changed back to brown while the nurse tended to his dad.

"I'll be back!" the nurse took off running.

Rico started to hyperventilate, drool shot everywhere, then Maria walked in there. She raced up to Rico and took his hands, but he was able to pull his hands away, "Honey, what's wrong?!"

"Shjinglin shjim! Shjingling Shjim!" is all he could say. His eyes were wide with fear, even the one that dropped seem to come alive with fear.

The nurse ran back in with a syringe and plunged it into Rico's leg. He fidgeted for a few more minutes then started to calm down, "I think we need to him back in bed."

"I understand Maurice, I don't know what happened." Maria said, tears in her eyes.

"Hopefully, he will be better for you next weekend, I'll let his doctor know what happened and hopefully she will figure something out," Maurice said and wheeled Rico away, who was back in a vegetative state.

"Thank you!" Maria said.

"Yes, thank you!" Richard followed up.

"I don't know what happened Richard, he's never done that before," Maria said wiped what tears were left in her eyes away.

"Maybe he will be better next weekend, maybe seeing me was too much for him," Richard said and looked saddened.

"No, I don't think that was it, he hasn't spoken in a long time. This was something else I feel."

"Let's just wait and see what the doctor says. I'm hungry though, should get grab something to eat while we are in town? I'll pay," Richard asked.

"I could use a margarita," Maria smiled and laughed.

"Then let's go get you one, I'll even drive home."

They left and drove south a little, there was city there that had a nice, authentic Mexican restaurant. It was a family-owned place, so they put the extra work in to make the food extra good. That parking lot there was fuller than the visiting parking lot at LaRuse Del Carto.

The building was just a small, beige painted, building with a stucco texture to it.  The roof had a red, clay tile shingles, that were arched over.  The door was wooden, square, and large enough to get a wheelchair through.  There was an outdoor seating area with a canopy over it for rainy days.  Bright, neon green lights lit up under the eve of the roof.  Fake palm trees were placed by the entrance along with a whimsical, four-foot beer bottle, with arms, legs, goofy large eyes, and a smile.

The inside was low-lit, with red, purple, white, and green lights around the top perimeter of the inside of the building.  There were no center tables, all booths, all the way around.  They took one along the wall about halfway down and sat down.  A few minutes later a waiter came up to them.

"Hi, I'm Levi, I'll be your waiter today, what can I start you off with?" he said.  He was medium-height and thin, had long hair, down to his shoulders.  His Adam's apple was prominent, and he had the faintest hint of a mustache on his upper lip.

"Well, Levi, I will have a large cherry cola to start and I haven't decided what I want yet to eat," Richard said.

Levi jotted it down, "and for you?" he looked at Maria.

"I'll have the seventy-four-ounce margarita and I should be ready to order when you come back," Maria said.

"Alright, I'll get those for you and chips with salsa are on the way," he said and walked away.

It was but a minute later that another man came up with two baskets of chips and two bowls of salsa and sat them down.  Richard and Maria looked at the menu and picked out their lunches, all the while snacking on chips and salsa.  The waiter came back ten minutes later with their drinks.  The margarita came in a large, clear glass.  The margarita was lime green in color, with a cherry floating in the center and salt littered the rim of the glass.

"Are you two ready to order?" the waiter asked.

"Yes," Maria said, "I'll have the number-7 combo, two tamales, a side of refried beans with sour cream and queso on top please."

"I'll have the burrito loco, extra shrimp, extra steak in it. A side of pintos and cheese and three steak chalupas," Richard said and sat the menu down.

"Okay, I'll that out to you as soon as possible," the waiter said and picked up the menus, then left.

It was less than half an hour later their food arrived and they were able to enjoy a nice lunch together. They chatted about the day's events, omitting Rico's weird behavior. Maria was a little tipsy, so of course, Richard drove home. Maria went and lay down. while Richard got to thinking about the articles he had read about the gardens. Whatever was ailing him lately took a break that day. One name was Mr. Helsir. He wanted to look more into him, so he remembered he had a friend on the police force, so he called in a favor.

"Heyyy Officer Thompson, its Richard Ruiz!" Richard spoke into the phone.

"Hey Ruiz! How are you?" Officer Thompson spoke. His voice was slightly raspy from years of smoking, but deep as well, he planned on quitting before he was forty, so he had two years more to go.

"I need to call in a favor, the owner of The Gardens, Mr. Helsir," Richard said.

"Yes what about him?"

"Can you find out about him, where he's from and what not, I got weird feeling about him," Richard said.

"Alright, I'll see what I can do, but now you owe me," Officer Thompson chuckled.

"That I do my friend," Richard said and they hung up.

Richard was rather tired after he got off the phone and decided to lay down for a while.  He didn't know he was going to crash from lack of sleep and was soon dead to the world.

## Chapter Twelve: Monday and Mrs. Peeley

Richard didn't wake up until two hours before his alarm. He thought he was going to feel well rested, he thought he wasn't going to feel all achy, but he was dead tired still.  He made some coffee and drank a cup.  He noticed an ache coming from his right canine. He went into the bathroom and looked in the mirror at his tooth.  It was brown, he touched it with his tongue and it shot pain through his jaw and up into his right eye.

"Holy hell!" Richard said and cringed in pain.  He reached up with his pointer finger and thumb and grasped the tooth.  He didn't know what he was thinking, but he started to pull down.  His eyes filled with tears, but he couldn't stop pulling.  There was pressure, a popping sound then the release of the pressure and the tooth came out and blood filled his mouth.  He spat the blood out in the sink and there was a large blood clot that came with it.

He rinsed all the blood down the drain. He held his tooth up to examine it.  It had never given any problems before but it looked like it had been rotted a long time, he then tossed his tooth in the trash.  He put his tongue in the socket hole and wiggled it around. He didn't bother brushing his teeth or showering.  He then left for work.

The moon was full that night as he rode his bike, he was staring at it while riding and almost ran into a car.  The heat subsided a little, but it still lingered even in the night.  He spotted Ron the minute it he turned in. He put his bike up and walked to the door.

Ron was waiting for him with a stressed look on his face, but smiled through it anyways, "Hey man! How was your weekend?" he asked as he opened the door.

"Went by way too fast," Richard said, "yours?"

"Same!" Ron said as they started walking towards the elevator, "Mrs. Peeley in E-twenty-two has been complaining about her bed."

They got on the elevator and started heading down, "What's wrong with her bed?" Richard asked.

"She wanted it lowered, which I lowered, but now she says it's too low and wants it raised back up.  I told her she will have to wait until tomorrow until we can bring in someone with a better understanding, but she's being difficult about it."

"Well most beds just have two heights, what's she expecting?" Richard said and tongued his tooth hole again.

"I don't know, like I said, some of the people here don't need to be here, she's one of them." He said.

The elevator opened and a smell of feces hit Richard right in the face, "Good god!" he said and shielded his nose with his hand.

"What?" Ron asked and looked confused.

"You don't smell that?" Richard asked, but when he removed his hand from his nose, he couldn't smell it anymore, "Well, never mind, it's gone now," Richard said and was more confused than Ron.

Ron went into his office and Richard went into his office and instantly noticed a floral smell, "What the hell?" he asked and looked around.  In a plug-in, next to the coffee maker was one of those scented plug-ins.  He reached over and unplugged it and tossed it in the trash.  He then opened up the fridge to get his coffee and there was another can of coffee in there besides his that was labeled "Decaf".  He then noticed a note on his coffee can.

"You should switch to decaf, it's better for you---Tiff." There was little heart on the note.  Richard grumbled a little as he crumbled the note up and tossed in in the trash.  He got in the cabinet where the coffee filters were at and found another kind in there as well. They were brown and read "Made from recycled materials." Richard shook his head, "Why would I want to filter my coffee through something made from recycled toilette paper? I can already tell I'm not going to like this girl."

He made his coffee and looked at the computer screens. He saw Dona walking fast, from one camera angle to the next. Michelle was at the nurse's station messing with her computer. Richard looked at the cameras in the garden area and at first, he could see someone standing in there by the rose garden. They had a walker, so he assumed it was one of the residents. They still had about fifteen minutes before he had to lock the garden doors. Richard looked away and when he looked back the person was gone. Richard clicked through some other angles to see if he could see the resident but there was nothing. Richard guessed the resident lived close to the garden and made it back to their room before he caught them.

Then came the nightly knock on the door and Richard walked Ron up to the sliding doors, let him out and locked it. When he turned around there were two people sitting on one of couches facing the large, T.V. hanging on the wall. He didn't see them when he came up and apparently neither did Ron. Richard didn't know who they were but he spoke up anyways.

"Hey, the lobby is closed," he said started walking up to them. He caught the faint smell of cigarette smoke. The one on the right had shorter hair and wore a leather jacket. The one on the left had blonde, shoulder length hair, but done up in an early eighties style and had on a nurse's hat. Richard thought they had done away with the nurse's hats, "Hey, I said the lobby is closed," he said a little louder, but the people still didn't move.

He walked up and put his hand on the nurse's shoulder, "Hey....." was all he could get out. The nurse's head tilted back and her eyes were wall white, they stared directly at Richard and then the head started tilting further back. Blood spewed from the neckline on the nurse as the head fell off backwards and bounced off Richard's feet. He screamed and walked backwards away from the head.  It stopped rolling and when it did, it was facing Richard with a sick, bloody smile on its face.

A small table next to a chair caught Richard behind the knee, causing him to fall over.  He fell hard on his back and knocked the wind out of him.  He let out a horrible gasp as he fought to take a breath.  After a minute or so, he was finally able to breathe, he got up in a hurry and looked over at the couch.  There was nothing there, no head, no blood, no bodies.

"God damnit Richard! Get your ass to the doctor or a Priest," Richard said, he took his hat off and rubbed his head.  He went back down and didn't even test the coffee in his cup, just dumped it and poured him a new one.  He found himself looking for sugar, he normally didn't like sugar in his coffee but he wanted it.  He started looking through the desk drawers and when he opened the center drawer, there was pack of cigarettes he had forgotten about, and of course, a note from Tiff.  He pulled the note off and put the cigarettes in his pocket. He searched some more and found a few, single, sugar packets.  He opened them and dumped them in his coffee, they'd work for the time being.

He left after that to go lock the garden doors.  The smell of feces hit his nose once more but went away after a while.  He walked by the nurse's station and stopped to chat with Michelle.

"Hey, do you keep smelling poop?" he asked.

"Honey, I smell poop all night long, welcome to my world," she joked.

"I just keep smelling it," Richard said and shook his head.  He headed to the dining room and moved all the chairs and tables into the closet.  He started down to the cleaning closet, grabbed the dust mop and headed back to the dining room.  He done a quick dust mop then got his machine.

For some reason that night he kept the curtains open while he scrubbed the floor.  He was making his final lap, when he decided to close the curtains, he was coming up close to the curtains with his machine, he looked up and suddenly a corpse appeared in front of him, on the other side of the window. Its right eye was hanging on by a thread of bloody nerves, half its skin was missing on its jaw and left orbital socket. Its hands were mostly bones and its clothes were in tatters.

The distraction caused Richard to run his machine into the wall, causing yet again, another hole in the wall, "Shit!" Richard said to himself, his heart started racing as he checked the damage.  It was just a small hole, but he knew Mark would have a fit over it.

"Don't ruin the machinery," he heard Dona say behind him.

"Shut up!" Richard said without looking back, he heard Dona huff, then scurry off.

He got up off his knees and reversed the machine, then finished his lap.  He looked again in the garden and there was nothing there. So, he shut the curtains and thought nothing more of it.  He took the machine out, parked it by the nurse's station and got glared at by Dona. He put the tables back, got the machine, and glared back at Dona as he walked by.  He dumped the water, refilled the machine and headed up to the lobby.  He was expecting to see the two bodies he had seen earlier, but they weren't there, thankfully.

He scrubbed the lobby without any more experiences, his shoes made a slight squeak as he done so.  He dumped the machine once more, rinsed it out and put it up for the night.  He then grabbed his trash cart and hit the west hall trash room.  He was on his way down to the east hall when he passed E-twenty-two and the door swung open.

In the doorway, stood Mrs. Peeley, no taller than five-foot. She had a pale blue, fuzzy robe, her white hair was in red, plastic curlers.  She had hate in her eyes and stared a hole through Richard.

"I need my bed fixed now, I can't sleep, it's too low to the ground," she snapped her voice was riddled with age.

"I don't see how being low to the ground effects your sleeping but I'm busy and you were already told it wouldn't be until tomorrow before it gets fixed," Richard said and started to move the cart.

"Well I was told at six o'clock yesterday and last time I looked," Mrs. Peeley looked at her watch, "it's after midnight so that means my bed will be fixed today," she smirked.

"Well he said today, last time I checked," Richard smirked back, "it's still nighttime, have a goodnight Mrs. Peeley," Richard said and walked away, pushing his cart towards the east hall even more.

He loaded up the trash and when he looked back, Dona was going into Mrs. Peeley's room, "Great!" Richard said and hurriedly pushed his cart towards the back dock. He loaded up the cart and the kitchen staff left an extra surprise for him of a fifty-five-gallon trash can, full of grease.

"Are you serious!?" Richard took the trashcan and wheeled it to the dock doors. He opened it and there was drain directly in front of the door and he dumped all the grease down the drain. He then took his cart and headed back towards west hall and hoped Dona wasn't there, but she was.

"Mrs. Peeley is complaining about her bed," Dona said.

"So, I'm security not maintenance, they'll fix it in the morning," Richard said and tried to get past Dona but she stood in his way.

"You need to fix it so she can rest, we have to go above and beyond for these residents," Dona said.

"Then you fix it," Richard said and shoved cart hard enough to make Dona move out the way.

"You're rude!" Dona mouthed as he walked by.

"If you say so."

Dona just stood there, blinking at Richard, she was used to getting her way and she wasn't with Richard.

Richard took the trash up and out to the compactor. As he was exiting the door, he reached down and grabbed the pack of cigarettes from his shirt pocket. He flipped them open the box top and looked in.  One cigarette was flipped opposite of the rest, with tobacco side up.  Tucked into the side of the pack, between the cigarettes and box were a pack of matches.  Richard took a cigarette out, but not the odd one, put it in his mouth and lit it up.  He took a long drag off it as he walked up to the compactor.  He let the smoke fill his lungs then exhaled out his nose.

Richard threw the trash in and waited until the compactor was done smashing the trash, finished his cigarette, then flipped the butt.  It bounced off the compactor, glared a bright red before falling to the ground.  He took the trash cart back down and as he was passing the nurse's station, he heard Michelle's voice.

"Hey! On your way back, can you stop back here please!" she said with a look of desperation in her eyes.

"Yeah, I will," Richard said, he put the cart away and headed back up to the nurse's station and tapped on the window.  Michelle pressed the button so she could speak.

"Will you please take a look at Mrs. Peeley's bed, please! I know its not your job, but Dona won't stop harassing me and neither will Mrs. Peeley. I will owe you one."

Richard took a deep breath and fought back what he wanted to say.  He shut his eyes and once again they turned grey, but Michelle didn't notice it, because she was typing stuff into a computer, "Yeah, I'll go take a look at it."

Richard went and knocked on Mrs. Peeley's door.  It was well past two in the morning, so he was hoping she would be asleep and he wouldn't have to mess with it.  She opened the door though, with the same anger in her eyes as earlier.

"It took you long enough, I'm filing a complaint in the morning, this is ridiculous," Mrs. Peeley said.

"The names Richard Ruiz, make sure you spell my name right," Richard sneered.

Mrs. Peeley glared, then moved out of the way so Richard could come in. Her apartment was nicely set up, not a thing was out of place. The recliner was set up at a perfect angle with the T.V. hanging on the wall. The carpet was clean, the trash cans empty, even the bedroom was immaculate. The white and rose bedspread was neat, not a wrinkle in sight, pillows looked as if they'd been untouched.

"What seems to be the problem?" Richard asked.

"Don't you remember what I told you earlier, my bed needs to be raised. It was too high, then it got lowered too low. I didn't think it would be that hard to fix a bed. Where'd they hire you people from, the funny farm?" she barked.

"Well, if it's so easy, you should be able to do it yourself then?" Richard barked back.

"I beg your pardon!?" she said and put her hand on her chest.

"You have such an opinion of me and an idea on how this should be done, you must have done it yourself before? Or are you no better than anyone else from the "funny farm" as you put it?"

"You get out of my room!" Mrs. Peeley pointed her arthritic finger at Richard.

Something in Richard shifted, he smiled and when he did, it scared Mrs. Peeley so bad she stumbled backwards, fell and hit her head off her dresser. She then hit the floor and something popped. She didn't get up after she hit the floor, she just laid there, with a dazed look on her face. Richard nudged her with his foot and she didn't move.

"Hmm," he said, "Want your bed raised do ya?" He moved her head closer to the corner of the bed, crudely with his foot.  He lifted the corner of the bed up, it was barely raised high enough to fit Mrs. Peeley's head under it.  There came a soft cracking sound, but Richard wasn't happy with it though.  So, he jumped up, and spun his backend around, plopping it on the corner of the bed.  A loud crunch came to his ears, and when he looked over the edge of the bed, he could see a puddle of blood forming from around the back of Mrs. Peeley's head. The leg of the bed was indented an inch into Mrs. Peeley's head.

"Bed seems high enough for me," Richard laughed and got up. He admired his work for a second then turned and left. He left Mrs. Peeley's room with no remorse whatsoever, but he did leave with a plan.

He was met by Dona the minute he walked out of the room, "Did you get her bed fixed?" Dona asked and once again, blocked Richard's way.

"Yes and she's resting comfortably and doesn't want to be bothered for the rest of the night."

"Could have saved some time and done it earlier," Dona said and narrowed her eyes at Richard.

"Don't you have a diaper to change?" Richard bumped into her, "next time you step in front of me, I won't stop."

Dona stormed off and when Richard passed the nurse's station, Michelle mouthed, "Thank you!" to him.  Richard went into his office and sat down.  He warmed up some coffee in the microwave then plopped down in his chair and waited for the second trash run.

The wait dragged, and he often felt himself going in and out of consciousness. He felt like something from within was pulling him into a darkness of sorts.  He decided he needed Mr. Latrell before the week was over.

It finally came time for the trash run.  He got his cart and was happy that Dona had filled up the west hall trash.  He stopped at E-twenty-two, looked around and opened the door, he then pushed the cart into her living room.

He lifted the bed off Mrs. Peeley's head, and brain matter stuck to the leg of the bed.  Richard took Mrs. Peeley and put her in the trash cart, she was the right height to fit perfectly in there.  He opened the door and looked down the hall and no one was in sight, so he pushed the cart out quickly and hurried down east hall to get the trash from there.  There wasn't as much, but enough that he could cover Mrs. Peeley and take her to the compactor.

He started walking down the hall and turned down the hall leading to the elevator when Dona came out from behind the nurse's station, Richard moved faster, trying to get away from her.  She picked up her pace as well to try to catch up with Richard.  He reached the elevator, swiped his badge, and pushed the buttons repeatedly.  Finally, the elevator doors opened and he shoved the cart in and got in. He pressed the buttons on the inside of the elevator as Dona closed in.  The doors started to close as Dona spoke up, "I need to talk to you when..." then the doors shut and Richard didn't hear the rest of what she said.

He took the cart out to the compactor.  He opened the door, reached in and took some of the compacted trash back out.  He took Mrs. Peeley's body and tossed her into the compactor, he then put in half the trash. He lit another cigarette and puffed on it while the air around stuck to him from the humidity.

He pressed the button and machine started working with a loud whine. It took a few seconds but he heard the bone crunching that he was waiting for, then came a wet, squishing sound.  The compactor rumbled to a stop and reversed, then Richard loaded up the second round of trash and crushed it as well.  He took his cigarette and flipped it off the compactor and smiled.

He went back down and managed to avoid Dona, he put his cart up and grabbed the carpet extractor, some bleach, peroxide and a rag.  He once again, managed to avoid Dona as he made to Mrs. Peeley's room undetected.  He moved the bed slightly over and used the extractor to clean up the blood off the carpet.  He used the rag and bleach to clean the brain matter off the leg of the bed.  Once he was done, he couldn't tell there had ever been a blood stain.

He opened the door and peeked out. No one was in sight, so he took the extractor back into the cleaning room and emptied it down the drain.  He watched as the bloody water swirled and some smaller pieces of brain disappeared down the drain.  He cleaned the extractor out with bleach and put the machine up for the night.

He was worried the cameras caught him going into Mrs. Peeley's room, so he looked.  He figured they wouldn't have a reason to look, but they'll notice Mrs. Peeley gone in the morning and might want to look at them.  So, he sat down and searched the cameras. Strangely enough it showed him doing his trash run, then going to his office.  He rewound it and watched it again, this time, halfway down the hallway he stopped and turned his head towards the camera, but it wasn't him, he didn't do that.  Then he winked at the camera and went on his way.  When Richard watched the tape for a third time, he didn't stop and wink.

"I think I need more coffee," Richard said and sighed "Or an exorcism." He brewed another fresh pot of coffee. He poured a cup before it was done, letting the coffee sizzle off the hotplate before putting the pot back. He took a big swig of the coffee, letting it scorch his throat all the way down.  He finished the cup and rinsed it out. He looked at the time and it was almost quitting time.  He cleaned out his coffee pot, and waited until it was time to let Doug in.

Once again, Doug wasn't there, so Richard went back down and watched as Doug showed up finally and walked up to the nurse's station.  He watched as Doug and Dona talked and then Michelle came into the equation.  Then there came a knock on the door.

"Hey, how was your weekend?" Mark asked, and seemed more cheerier than normal.

"Mine was fine, how was yours?" Richard asked, omitting the fact he hit the wall and left a hole.

"Drank a few, here and there," he smiled.

"Not much happened last night," Richard lied and smiled.

"That's what I like to hear."

Mark went into the maintenance office and shut the door. Richard shut his door, sat down for a few more minutes and then clocked out.  He knocked on the Mark's door and when Mark opened it, he bid him a good day and went home.

There was a slight breeze that morning, Richard took his shirt off and let his pits air dry, so to speak.  Breakfast wasn't set out when he got home, and he skipped out on the shower again.  He simply went and laid down and tried to sleep.

## **Chapter Thirteen: Tuesday and Mr. Bilbey**

Richard didn't sleep at all, he lay awake the whole day, replaying in his head, what he had done. He didn't want to remember, but he was this time.  The thing that bothered him most was he didn't feel bad about it either.  He just stared at the ceiling fan above his bed, watching it twirl around.  He got to thinking about everything he had seen so far and didn't want to go to work, then heard a voice.

"You're gotta go kiddo, you got work to do, they don't respect you, you gotta make them respect you," it was Jingling Jim's voice and it was in his head.

"They respect me, they just have their own stuff going on and don't really show it," Richard said.

"You're full of shit kiddo, that Dona is always telling you what to do, like she owns the place," his voice got sharp, "Michelle makes fun of you when you're not around, I know because I'm always around, I'm everywhere."

"Please, I know what my dad did, I know he shoved you in the incinerator, he's paid for it ever since. I just want to be left alone," Richard pleaded, his heart started racing.

"Nah, I have unfinished business with this place, and since your dad cut that short, you're going to have to finish what I started," Jingling Jim said.

Richard shot up out of bed and went into the bathroom and looked in the mirror. For a split second his face wasn't his face, it was mix of his face and Jingling Jim's. He screamed and punched the mirror, shattering it.

"RICHARD RUIZ! WHAT ARE IN THERE BREAKING?'

"I slipped momma and hit the mirror, I'm fine," he said.

"I KNOW YOU'RE FINE, NOTHING CAN HURT THAT HEAD OF YOURS!" Maria laughed.

Richard rolled his eyes and looked at his hand, a few knuckles were cut, but it was nothing too horrible.  He washed the blood off his hands and went to try to lay back down for an hour or so to try to get some sleep.  It didn't happen, Jingling Jim's voice was in his head.  His alarm finally went off and he rolled out of bed.

He brushed his teeth and when he spit out the toothpaste, it was tainted red with blood.  He grabbed the mouthwash and it was in instant burn when he gurgled it.  The mouthwash was tainted as well when he spit it out.  He didn't shower once again, nor put on deodorant.  He got on his bike and pedaled to the gas station where he bought more energy drinks.  He was wearing the same outfit that wore the night before and found the cigarettes in the front pocket.  He lit one up as he got on his bike, the cherry of cigarette glowed a bright orange as he pedaled.

Richard didn't even lock his bike.  He simply jumped off it and let it crash into the bike rack.  He was fighting being him, as he weakened, Jingling Jim took over. He needed to see Mr. Latrell. He took his cigarette out his mouth and flipped off onto the concrete. Ron was waiting for him and gave him an odd look as he unlocked the door.

"I didn't know you smoked," Ron said.

"There's a lot you don't know about me, kiddo!" Richard said and brushed by Ron, "Anything happen tonight?"

"Yeah, Mr. Bilbrey won't come out of the garden.  He keeps going back in and was there last time I checked."

"Great! Another one that doesn't belong here I take it?" Richard asked.

"He's usually sound, but tonight he didn't want to leave the garden.  He said for what he pays to live here, he should be able to visit the garden whenever he wants."

"Well, he can't, I have to lock it at eleven-thirty, so he will have to get out by then."

"I hope you have better luck than I did," Ron said.

"I will," Richard smiled.

Richard went into his office, made a half a pot of coffee, then added the two energy drinks to the rest of the coffee, "That should do it," he said smiled and let it warm up, then poured him a cup.

He went in the dining room and could see Mr. Bilbrey wandering around the garden.  He tapped on the window and pointed to his wrist to let Mr. Bilbrey know he was on a time limit. Mr. Bilbrey had age spots on his bald head, no glasses, but walked as if he could hardly see and wore brown slippers.  He had on a baby-blue shirt, with khaki pants.  He looked at Richard and flipped him off.

"Very nice Mr. Bilbrey thank you for that," Richard said and headed up to let Ron out.  He told Ron to have a goodnight and then headed towards the garden.  He stopped at Mr. Latrell's room but heard Dona in there, so he continued heading towards the garden.

He walked in and found Mr. Bilbrey standing by the roses, "Mr. Bilbrey its time to get out of the garden, I have to lock it up for night."

"Screw off, dickweasel!" Mr. Bilbrey said.

"You need to get out!" Richard raised his voice.

"You need to eat my ass!" Mr. Bilbrey said and stumbled a little bit.

Richard threw his hands up in the air and walked out.  He walked up to Michelle and pressed the button on the intercom, "Hey, I'm going to wax and buff the floors tonight. Mr. Bilbrey has until I'm done with the dining room then I'm locking him in."

Michelle spun around and she looked worn out already, "You okay?" he asked.

"Mrs. Peeley got out between night and first shift, but she wasn't picked up on any of the cameras and for some reason, I'm getting blamed for it," Michelle said, teary-eyed.

"Hmm, I figured they would have called me," Richard said and pulled out his phone.  He looked at it and saw he had four missed calls, from Sheila, "I'll be damned, I didn't even hear my phone go off. I'm sure they will figure it out sooner or later, I can vouch for you if needed."

"Would you?" Michelle smiled.

"Yeah of course, but like I said, I'm going to wax the dining room and he will have to be out, I'm already going to be in trouble for locking it late."

"I will try to get him out when you do," Michelle said and wiped a tear from her eye, "If not, Ativan!" she smiled.

"Thank you!"

Richard took and put all the tables and chairs up, then went and got the scrubber.  He noticed on his way around scrubbing that the hole was still in the wall.  He made a few, quick laps to scrub up any loose debris and then went and got the wax.  He only put on one coat this time, then turned the fans on the wax to help it dry.  He turned around and Dona was standing just beyond the wax line. He walked up to her with the mop bucket.

"Do all those fans need to be running? They're loud!"

"Yes, they help dry the wax, so I can buff the floor later."

"I'm going shut a few off!" Dona said.

"No, you're not, you can't walk across the floor the wax is still wet!" Richard said and stopped Dona from entering the dining room,

"Don't you have a resident you need to get out of the garden? Or does he gets locked in there?"

Dona stood there, Richard could tell by the way she was looking at him, she didn't like being told what to do.  She scuffed and walked off, Richard laughed to himself as he pushed the wax bucket down the hall.  He cleaned up the bucket, knowing he still had the lobby to do, and walked out of the room.

"Mr. Bilbrey won't come out, there's not much I can do," Dona said.

"I guess I'll have to take care of him myself," Richard said and walked by Dona.

He found Mr. Bilbrey by roses again and called out to him, "Mr. Bilbrey, it's time to go."

"Nope, don't believe I will!" he said and stared at the roses.

"I have to lock it up Mr. Bilbrey," he said and walked up to Mr. Bilbrey, Mr. Bilbrey then took a swing at Richard, but missed, "Whoa!" Richard said and without thinking, lunged at Mr. Bilbrey and grabbed his head.  Black tendrils shot out of Richard's fingers and dug into the head of Mr. Bilbrey.  Richard's eyes turned grey and Mr. Bilbrey let out a strange moan.

Images flashed in Mr. Bilbrey's head of all the victims Jingling Jim and Richard had killed.  Blood filled scenes of murder and dismemberment. Mr. Bilbrey's eyes grew wide and the blood vessels started to burst, his tongue stuck out and down to the left of his mouth.  Richard pulled his hands away and the black tendrils retreated into his hands. Mr. Bilbrey stumbled back and sat down on the edge of the rose bed, a dumbfounded look on his face, his left eye, and lip slightly drooped down.

"Guess you need a nurse!" Richard smiled and walked out to find Michelle, she was coming from the elevator, "Hey! Something is wrong with Mr. Bilbrey, I was talking to him and he got dizzy, then I had to help him sit down, he' s not acting right."

"Okay, I'll come check him out," she said and Richard led her to Mr. Bilbrey.

He was still sitting in the same spot, same look on his face. She asked his name a few times and only got a blank stare in return, "I think he's had a stroke, can you go grab me wheelchair?" Michelle asked.

"Yeah, not a problem," Richard said and went to a small closet next to the nurse's station and grabbed a wheelchair.  He walked hurriedly back and brought the wheelchair up next to Mr. Bilbrey.

"Get under his arm and help me transfer him," Michelle demanded, "I would have rather of given him Ativan," Michele joked.

Richard laughed and done as he was told, he didn't like being bossed, but Michelle had been good to him, so he didn't mind. Michelle counted to three and they lifted Mr. Bilbrey and put him into the wheelchair.  Michelle pushed him out of the garden area and Richard locked the doors with a smile on his face.

"And just like that, I get to do my job," Richard said and doubled checked his lock job.

He went up and scrubbed the lobby and done a single coat of wax after that and had the floor looking good, when he noticed and ambulance pull up in front of the building, "Are you serious?" he asked himself as he was standing by elevator.

They knocked on the door and he pointed to the right, which would lead them to the ramp that leads to the dock.  They knocked again and repeated the gesture.  He then went down and out the dock, then up the ramp.  He could still see the paramedics standing at the front entryway.

"Bunch of morons," he said quietly, "HEY! THIS WAY!" he yelled and caught their attention.

One of them, a male, rather tall and bulky and whose paramedic shirt was two sizes, too small, shook his head.  The other paramedic was also a male, who was short and skinny, he pulled the gurney while the other one walked briskly towards Richard.

"What's going on up front?" the bulky male asked. Richard was able to get a better look at him once he was up close.  He was dark in color, had brown eyes and angry look. His jawline was broad and square with the corner of lips, seemingly, permanently turned down.  Even in the low light Richard could see the veins in guy's arms.

"I just waxed the floor and don't want it walked on," Richard said and looked at the paramedic.

"Can't you just rewax it?" the paramedic remarked.

"No, I can't, I didn't think a person of your stature would have issues walking a few measly steps," Richard pipped back.

"Come on Tommy, hurry up!" the paramedic yelled to the other one, who was struggling to push the gurney by himself.

Tommy finally made it there and had even more trouble coming down the ramp with the gurney.  Richard led them through the kitchen and down the hall to where Michelle had Mr. Bilbrey waiting.  They transferred him to the gurney and Dona started leading them towards the elevator.

"You can't go that way Dona, the wax is drying," Richard said.

Dona turned around and simply smirked at Richard, he was ready to say something when Michelle called out to him, "I need you to fill out some paperwork."

"Okay DONA! DON'T GO THAT WAY!" Richard yelled.

Dona stopped and the angry paramedic said something to her and she chuckled.

Richard followed Michelle behind the nurse's station where he spent ten minutes filling out the paperwork, simply because he was there when Mr. Bilbrey had his "stroke".  He had to lie about some things, like what signs he was having, did he lose color, etc.

After he got done, he looked up and saw Dona coming up the hallway with a smile on her face.

"Damnit!" Richard said and raced from behind the nurse's station, "I swear to god Dona, if you walked across that floor…"

"You won't do shit, I run this show," she said and walked by Richard almost bumping into him.

He raced to the elevator and couldn't swipe his badge and press the buttons fast enough.  The ride up was excruciatingly slow, but when the doors opened, Richard wished they wouldn't have.  His heart picked up pace and he could feel the blood rush to his face.  There, leading from the elevator doors, through the lobby, and stopping at the front doors, were tracks from the gurney and footprints.

"That bitch!" Richard said and went back downstairs.  He grabbed painters' tape, wax stripper and a mop bucket. "So much for seeing Mr. Latrell tonight!" he said to himself.

He went up and taped off three inches away from the outside footprints, the total area was four-feet wide by sixty-feet long.  He put down the stripper, making sure to keep it inside the tape lines.  He made sure to start at the at the front doors and work towards the elevator.  He made sure he didn't step in the stripper.  He let it sit and while he let it sit, he went and got the scrubber.  He only added little water to the machine, then took it up.  He made sure to start immediately when the doors opened. He kept the machine between the two blue, taped lines and when got close to the sliding doors, he stopped.  He walked to the side, leaned over, unlocked the doors, and hit the button to make them open.  He got back behind the scrubber and turned it around in the foyer and then scrubbed back to the elevator.

After bringing the machine down, he had to mix the wax mixture up again and headed back up to the lobby. He then put some wax down, running a line up and down the edges, then gently swaying back and forth, filling in the stripped spot with wax.  He moved the mop bucket in the elevator and then down to the cleaning room.  He rushed back to the elevator to see Dona smirking at him from behind the nurse's station.  He went and stood by the elevator until thirty minutes had passed.  He went back up, and pulled the tape and then smiled.  He couldn't tell there was ever an area that was messed up. He was rather proud of his work.

He rushed back down, cleaned up the mop bucket and scrubber then sat half the tables back out.  He went back, heated up his coffee and energy drink mixture, then reviewed some parking lot footage.  He rewound all the way until he saw Dona come in, then looked to see what vehicle she drove.  It was a little red, chevy s10 with flare sides.

He took his box cutter and headed back upstairs.  He didn't have a lot of time, so he rushed out to Dona's truck.  He didn't flatten the tires, but cut a thin cut, at a diagonal, it looked deep, but it wasn't deep enough to puncture the tires.  They'd expand when she drove and pop when least expected.  It wasn't something Richard has done, but Jingling Jim has before.  Richard raced back inside and waited for Doug to pull in.

He watched a red Corvette pull into the lot and Doug was behind the wheel.  They made eye contact and Richard started laughing as he unlocked the door and pressed the button to activate them.  He went into his office and finished his coffee, he didn't even care that it was cold and then heard the knock on the door.

"Hey, how'd it go last night?" Mark asked and adjusted his hat.

"I didn't get a second trash run in because Dona led the paramedics through a floor I just waxed," Richard said a little anger in his voice.

"I only have to see her for five minutes and she drives me nuts," Mark said, "What were medics here for?"

"Oh yeah, Mr. Bilbrey had a stroke in the garden by the rose garden."

"Well, that sucks, they're dropping like flies around here."

"That's life for ya I guess!"

"I guess, well you have a good day!"

"You too!"

Mark went to his office and shut the door. Richard clocked out, shut out the lights to his office, then shut the door.  He looked back and Dona was standing at the beginning of the hallway, looking down.  He smiled and went up the elevator, admired his floor once more and then headed outside.

He picked his bike up off the ground, lit a cigarette and took a different way home, he went down to a house that had long been abandoned.  He felt like had seen the house before but he hadn't. He didn't even know it existed until he rode up on it.

## **Chapter Fourteen: Wednesday, the Call, and Dona**

Dona was on her way home, rushing in and out of traffic, cutting people off. She was racing down interstate-65 well above the speed limit. She was blaring her music and getting ready to turn on an exit to head into Columbus, Indiana, when her front two tires blew. Naturally being in a constant state of panic mode, Dona panicked even more. She jerked the wheel too hard to the right, the truck turned, skidded, then flipped.

Glass shattered all around, a sound of metal bending could be heard by Dona as she was tossed about. She saw the sun and sky, then pavement, then sun again, and finally pavement. She was upside down, then blacked out. When she woke up, she had warm, sticky fluid coming from her mid-section, up her chin and dripping off onto her forehead. She had immense pain coming from her stomach, she looked and could see a metal post from a road sign, sticking through her mid-section and into her truck seat.

Oil and gas oozed out of the truck, Dona could smell the gas and screamed out for help. She heard a vehicle brake and come to a screeching halt. She heard footsteps, then saw a pair of red, leather work boots appear next to her.

"Hey! Hey! Are you okay?" a male asked, then a face appeared. A man in is forties with a brown and white beard, a red and black flannel shirt, and a ball cap, stuck his head through the window a little to look, "Oh shit!" he said as he saw the metal post that impaled Dona to her seat, "Hold on, I'm going to call for help."

Dona nodded, it was all she could do, the blood rushing to her head was starting to make her dizzy. She heard the guy that was trying to help her yell out, then the concerning sound of another vehicle braking hard. The sounds of tires squealing, more metal crunching and glass shattering filled her ears. Her car suddenly jolted forwards, snapping her head back. The last images Dona saw, was her hood causing a spark between the concrete and metal, igniting a flame. The flame rushed towards Dona, burning her eyelids off, then the car burst into flames and Dona was no more.

Richard was sitting up in his bed, staring at the ceiling when an image of Dona's flesh burning off her face, popped in his head. He started smiling then started laughing a sinister laugh. He heard his mom ruffling around, then stopped laughing and listened. He heard no more movement, then his phone vibrated, he looked at it, it was Officer Thompson.

"Hey, what's up?" Richard asked.

"Well, I done some digging on Mr. Helsir and I came to find out, he didn't really exist up until about five years ago," Officer Thompson said.

"Really?"

"Yeah, and here's another strange thing. Two years before, to the exact date that Mr. Helsir, popped up, a missing person report was filed for none other than Johnathon McCurdy, Jim McCurdy's son. Might not be related, but just seem its odd. I mean Johnathan disappears, then two years later Mr. Helsir pops up and renovates The Gardens, the same place that Johnathan's father burnt down."

"That is a little weird, it's a little to coincidental not to be related."

"That's what I'm thinking, I'm going to dig a little deeper and see what I can find."

"That sounds good, keep me posted," Richard said.

"Will do, talk at ya later!" Officer Thompson said and hung up.

Richard shut his eyes and tried to get to some sleep, but once again, he had nightmares and tossed and turned most of the day. At some point he was actually getting sleep, then a neighbor started mowing grass. Richard rolled over and looked at his clock, it was six in the afternoon. He put his pillow over his face and screamed into it, then decided to get up.  He didn't shower again, or brush his teeth, just simply sat up in his bed, watching the time get closer for time to go to work.

He got up, put on an unwashed uniform, that still housed his pack of cigarettes.  He grabbed his bike and sat on it a second.  He then lit one up and started riding towards the gas station with a lit cigarette in his mouth.  As he rode the end of the cigarette lit up a bright orange.  He bought his normal energy drinks, lit up another cigarette and headed to work.  He was gentler with his bike this time. He flipped the cigarette again at the side of the wall and watched it bounce off.

Ron wasn't at the door this time and Richard pulled on it a few times.  He took his keys out and unlocked the doors himself, which were hard to push open without the button being pressed. He shut them back and locked them, then headed down the elevator. When it opened there stood Ron, pale as can be, sweat rolling off his brow, his eyes wide as can be.

"I'm so sorry, I had an emergency to deal with, the funeral home will be here later," Ron said, as he wiped the sweat from his brow.

"It's fine, I'm not late, but what happened?"

"Mr. Alco in E-Twelve, tripped and landed on a small trashcan, it shattered and a sharp piece cut his throat.  There was so much blood, every ounce in his body was on his living room floor.  It took me a couple hours to get the blood sucked up and another hour to get the carpet looking good." Ron said as they walked towards their offices.

"Why couldn't he have fallen in the kitchen, at least it's tile, been able to mop it up," Richard said and smiled.

"I wish he wouldn't had fallen at all," Ron said and stared, he shook his head and went into his office. Ron crinkled his nose, he could smell Richards body odor, it was bad.

Richard clocked in, made his half coffee and half energy drink concoction, then headed up to shut the curtains, when he saw Michelle on the phone and worried look on her face. He walked up and pecked on the window and she put up her finger to signal him for to hold on. She hung up the phone and came out of the nurse's station.

"Well, you won't have to worry about Dona anymore. She died in a car crash this morning, a really horrible one from what I was just told," Michelle said and look disturbed.

"Well that sucks, wonder what caused it?"

"I don't know, they won't be able to tell either, her truck went up in flames, they only knew it was Dona because of a few personal belongings that flew out and the license plate didn't burn."

"She always was a little fiery, guess her actions caught up to her," Richard chuckled.

"I know you didn't like her, but even that's low!" Michelle said and rolled her eyes, then turned around and walked away from the intercom.

Richard walked over and pressed the button to close the curtains, then walked down and locked the garden doors. He walked back and met Ron as Ron was coming out of his office. Richard walked him up and locked the doors, then went down and drank some of his mixture.

He reviewed the tapes and rewound them until he saw a second shift person come out of E-Twelve in a rush and came back with some help. Then he saw another person, who looked like the second-shift nurse come out, covered in blood, and run down the hall. He came back with trashcans and Ron was right behind him. Ron went into the room then came out quickly and threw up. Richard laughed at the sight, then rewound it and watched it again.

"What a puss!" he said and watched as some time went by before Ron came back with the carpet extractor and it took Ron five trips before he quit going to the room, "Damn, I missed all the action."

A flash of lights caught Richard's attention as a minivan pulled up that Richard recognized as the funeral homes.  He went up and met the worker, it was different one this time. A tall, skinny boy, maybe the age of eighteen, with combed over, long black hair.  He had a deep voice when he spoke.

"I'm Kenny, I'm here to pick up a body," he said and attempted a smile.

"Well, I'm sure you are," Richard said, "Follow me!"

Richard led Kenny down to E-Twelve and on the way down Kenny asked in his baritone voice, "Do you know what happened?"

"Resident tripped and landed on a plastic trashcan, a sharp piece slit his throat, he bled out before they could save him.  Took the second-shift maintenance a couple hours to clean up the mess," Richard said.

"That kinda sounds cool!"

"Doesn't it?" Richard looked back, "I'm sad I missed it."

"Wish I could have seen that."

"I like you kid, I hope you stick around," Richard said and smiled.

"I hope so too, I want to run my own funeral parlor."

"I think you will one day," Richard said and patted Kenny's shoulder.

The elevator opened and Richard led Kenny to the room where the body was waiting on the bed in the bedroom, "Think you can help we with this?" Kenny asked.

"Yeah sure, not a problem," Richard said and grabbed the feet of Mr. Alco as Kenny grabbed the shoulders.  They hoisted Mr. Alco onto the gurney, then Kenny sipped up the body bag.

Richard was leading Kenny back out when Michelle stopped him, "Hey, here in about an hour, I need you to let my CNA in, she usually works dayshift, but wanted nights.  Her name is Leola."

"Not a problem!"

"What a way to start a shift let me tell ya!"

"This place isn't doing so well," Richard joked.

"You got that right."

Michelle went back to the nurse's station and Richard finished taking Kenny back out.  He then went down and moved all the tables and scrubbed half of the floors before it was time to go let Leola in.  He was hoping he'd have time to talk to Mr. Latrell that night.

Richard was whistling as he rode up in the elevator, he started walking up to the doors and stopped whistling.  Standing at the door was a female, with brown hair, and eyes, thick from waist down.  She was the right height for Richard's liking, just coming up to his chin.  She had her hair pulled back in a ponytail, but it was more at the top than the back of the head.  She had the prettiest of smiles and little button chin.

Richard unlocked the doors and pressed the button to slide them open.  Leola spoke, "Hello, I'm Leola," her voice was soft and melted Richard's heart.

"I'm Richard, I'll take you down to Michelle."

"I wanted nightshift, but after seeing the track record for nightshift CNA's, I'm kind of worried."

"I think you'll do fine, just gotta remember you ain't nobodies' boss, Dona had a hard time with that and tried telling me what to do, please, don't do that." Richard pleaded.

"Oh I won't, I don't like drama and like to stay in my lane if you know what I mean?" her voice made his heart skip a beat.

"I do, same here, I just want to be left alone to do my job, work my eight and get out of here," Richard said.

"I think we will get along just fine," Leola said.

"I believe so as well."

Richard led her up to Michelle, who thanked him. Richard went back to scrubbing the floor with a smile on his face. He was happy he didn't have to deal with Dona ever again. He finished the dining room and put all the tables back. Every once and a while, he would catch Leola looking at him or the other way around. He then cleaned out the machine, then headed up to do the lobby. He had it down to a science and had it done in record time. He put up the machine and then went and made a trash round. He stopped at Mr. Latrell's door, knocked, then opened it, enough light came in, he could see Mr. Latrell was asleep, so he left him. He shut the door and headed on his way.

The hallways trash rooms weren't as full as when Dona was there, which told Richard, that Dona was overloading the trash on purpose. He was able to get to the kitchen, which is where he found a note from someone coming in, in the morning.

"Make sure you put liners back in the grease can and other trash bags, it makes my job easier."

Richard rolled his eyes and looked at the grease can, which was overfilled again. He simply took and dumped down the drain by the ramp. He didn't see the point in putting in liner and out of spite, didn't replace any other liner, in fact, he kicked a trash can over and left it.

He was on his way back up, when Leola stopped him, "I hope I didn't leave too much trash for you," she said.

"Nope, just enough to where I can make it in one trip, which I like," Richard smiled.

Leola smiled, but Richard could tell she caught a whiff of his body odor or breath. Leola then headed down west hall and Richard watched as she walked away. He took the trash up to the compactor, lit a cigarette and breathed in the moist air. Sweat started to form on his brow from the heat, he hated it. Heat lightning filled the sky, Richard was craving a rainstorm, but he had to settle with the moisture in the air.

He headed back in and sat down at his desk, reheated his mixture in the microwave and drank it down, "Ahhhhh! That hit the spot," he said after swallowing. He was scanning through the camera feed when a figure appeared outside of Mr. Alco's room. Richard looked and it was Mr. Alco, blood soaked his green shirt and beige pants. He was looking right at Richard, eyes blackened over.

"Oh no my friend, you died on your own accord, I had nothing to do with it," he said, but his voice was slightly different. Mr. Alco didn't move just stared as blood oozed down and onto the carpet, "You're making a mess Mr. Alco, go haunt somewhere else. Just because I wanted to see you die, doesn't mean I want you here anymore."

Mr. Alco started walking down the hall in a twitchy manner, but disappeared once he left the screen. Richard rubbed his eyes, "You're losing it man, you need sleep," he said, "I'm not going to let you sleep Richard," he said to himself in another voice, "We have unfinished business." Richard rubbed his temples, "No, you have unfinished business, I'm just somehow part of this."

Before Richard could say anything else there came a knock on the door. He opened it and there stood Leola, "Who are you talking to?" she smiled.

"Oh…um..it's something I do when I get tired. I create scenarios in my head and talk them out in different voices and drink this," he said and raised his cup.

"Coffee?"

"Coffee mixed with energy drink," he smiled and took a sip.

"That sounds gross!"

"Get you a cup, you'll like it," Richard said.

"I'm up for almost anything, but this I might have to draw the line on," she chuckled.

"Seriously, go get you cup," Richard told her and smiled again.

She disappeared for a second, then knocked again, when Richard opened it, Leola had a pink coffee cup. Richard poured some out in her cup and popped it in the microwave for a minute. The microwave beeped and he handed the cup to Leola. She was hesitant to try then finally did. She took a sip and she made a sour face, "That's really bad," she said and took another sip and smiled once more, "Anyway, Michelle needs to talk to you, she wants a favor I think."

"Okay, I'll be up in a minute, going to finish this first," Richard said and raised his cup.

"So if you're not up there in a few minutes, should I assume you're dead?" Leola laughed and walked away.

Ten minutes later, Richard emerged from his office and walked up to the nurse's station. Leola was still holding her mug as Richard tapped on the window, Michelle pressed the button and spoke, "You think on your second round of trash you could check my car for me?"

"What am I checking for?"

"Anything, I just think it's weird Dona dies on her way home, what if someone messed with her vehicle," Michelle said, the comment struck some fear in Richard.

"Well she wasn't very likeable, so I could see it. You on the other hand are very likeable, but if it makes you feel better, I'll give your car the once-over," Richard said and nodded at Michelle, "What time does Mr. Latrell wake up?"

"if he sleeps through the night, usually after you leave, why?"

"He's an ex-priest right?"

"Yes he is."

"Good, I just have a few questions from him, I might come in early and talk to him instead of waking him up."

"Please don't wake him up," Michelle laughed.

I won't, I'll wait!"

"Thank you!"

He went back to his office and waited for the second round of trash, nothing spooky happened on the cameras and Richard enjoyed a fourth cup of his mixture. He then went and got trash, he passed Leola in the hall and she had an earbud in her ear and was slightly singing to the music. Richard just smiled at her but she was in her own little world and went into a room.

He grabbed the trash, then stopped by the nurse's station and tapped on the glass to get Michelle's attention, she pressed the button and he talked, "What type of car do you drive?" he asked.

"A blue, Honda Civic, I park it in the middle row," she said.

"Alrighty!" he said and walked down east hallway and got the trash from there. It was like it was back before Dona, easy-peasy, one load trash runs.

Richard took the trash up and out the side door and to the compactor. He done his normal trash compacting, he smoked a few cigarettes and realized he was running low. After the trash compacted, he pushed the cart inside the door then walked to the parking lot. He was able to find the blue Honda rather easily. He didn't really check it over because he had no reason to. He just wanted to show up on camera in case Michelle asked to see it. He took the opportunity to smoke another cigarette, this time flipping it off Michelle's car.

He took the cart back in, took it to the cleaning room and carefully sprayed it out. He put it up then felt as if someone else was in the room with him. He could hear breathing then had sleep paralysis while he was awake. He heard the shuffling of feet and walking up behind him was the rotted corpse of one of the dead residents.

Their mouth as agape, their nose was rotted off, their skin a deathly hue of blue. The resident brought their boney fingers up and Richard could feel as they were placed on his shoulders, their cold grasp tightened. The jaws of the corpse started chattering, Richard could feel liquid on his neck as some slime-like drool came out of the mouth of the corpse, "Weeee willll havvvee ourrrr revvvveeeenge!" it said.

Richard closed his eyes and when he opened them he was able to move and there was no one else there in the room with him. He wiped at his neck where the drool had hit, and it was bone dry, "That's it, I'm buying sleeping pills after I get off work, I can't take this anymore," Richard said and rushed out of the room. He rushed past Leola and went into his office and shut the door. He didn't come out again until it was time to unlock the doors.

He was cleaning up the coffee pot when the normal knock came on the door. He opened it and there stood Mark and asked his normal question, "Anything go on last night?"

"Well, not last night, but yesterday Mr. Alco slipped and fell on a plastic trashcan, which slit his throat. Then Dona died in a car crash," Richard said and refrained from smiling.

"Well, sucks to be them," Mark said then suddenly stopped as if Richard was going to be offended.

"That's what I thought!" Richard laughed.

Mark went into his office and Richard went into his, clocked out and headed to Waltz, a local, twenty-four-hour supermarket. The big, grey, ominous building could be seen from miles away, the place was a necessary evil. It stood just outside of Yertzville, which made for a decent bike ride for Richard. Richard was out of breath by the time he got there, which was unusual for him.

He went in through the sliding, double doors. He was hit square in the face, with the sweet smell of doughnuts being made. There were aisles upon aisles of products, they had just started setting out Fourth of July items that caught Richard's eye as he walked past the five aisles of decorations and fireworks then headed towards the pharmacy.

He found the sleeping pill area and there were over, two-dozen different types of pills to choose from. There were also gummies and powders. Richard was overwhelmed and grabbed the bottles that were in the middle price range between the brands. He grabbed three bottles and went to a self-checkout so he could get out of there faster. After being carded, he swiped his card and got out of there as fast as he could. He was dreading the ride home.

He stopped a few times on his way home to catch his breath, but eventually made it home. His mom had breakfast ready, which consisted of eggs and chorizo, refried beans, tortillas, thick cut bacon, orange juice and milk. Richard wasn't particularly hungry, but feared the flip-flop, so he sat down and ate. His momma was nowhere in sight, she must have cooked then went to bed.

He ate the food and then washed the dishes, opted out of coffee and took four the sleeping pills and headed to bed. Before he went to sleep, he tried praying, which is something he hadn't done in a long time.

"Dear heavenly father, please, please protect me from this demon, give me the strength to get up and early and talk to Mr. Latrell, I need you and I'm sorry for not praying earlier, amen!" Richard said, he touched his shoulders, chest and head in a cross-like manner and went to bed.

## Chapter Fifteen: Thursday, Vivid Nightmares, Mrs.Faulson and Mr. Latrell

Richard's pills kicked in and he was able to get some sleep, but it wasn't long after he went to sleep that started dreaming.  He was at work, but it wasn't work, it was older, rundown, the drop ceiling was molded in spots and water dripped through the tile in others.  The carpet had bloodstains all over it and Richard could feel a slight crunch to it under his feet.  Lights flickered all around with a very audible, broken hum.

Richard could hear disembodied voices and see an orange, flickering light coming from the west hallway.  He proceeded up the hallway with caution.  He could feel his fear, he knew something was around the corner.  The voices echoed throughout the building as he walked.  A light fixture fell by the nurse's station, causing a spark.

Richard put his hand on the corner and slowly looked down west hall where the orange, flickering light was. At the end of west hall by the old incinerator was on fire.  A flame was shooting out of the wall, but nothing else was burning.  A sinister laugh broke out and Richard looked around for it, he saw no one, but when he turned back around to look down west hall, there stood Jingling Jim.

"You can't get rid of me boy! I'm part of you now, I will win this and finish what I started," Jingling Jim said and started walking towards Richard, his keys jingling with each step.

Richard ran towards the elevator, he felt like he was sinking into the floor.  The harder he tried to move the slower he moved.  The jingling picked up pace, Richard could feel Jingling Jim closing in, then at the last second, he worked himself free and raced up to press the elevator's buttons.

"You won't win this Jim, I will keep fighting and praying" Richard said, looking at Jingling Jim, who was just standing about five feet away with a smirk on his face.

"Are you sure about that?" Jingling Jim laughed, the prayer not only hurt Jingling Jim, it angered Jim greatly.

The elevator dinged and Richard turned around to board it when he noticed blood seeping out the elevator's door. The elevator opened and a massive wave of blood rushed out, surrounding Richard and carried him back towards Jingling Jim. Blood filled his mouth, it was bitter, he reached his hand out to grab onto something, anything. Someone grabbed onto him, and laughter could be heard once more. He was pulled up out of the blood and it was by Jingling Jim who was laughing maniacally, "I GOT YOU BOY!" he screamed.

Richard woke up screaming again, covered in sweat, "RICHARD, ARE YOU OKAY?" he heard his momma yell.

"YEAH, SLEEPING PILLS GAVE ME NIGHTMARES," he yelled back.

"OKAY!" she yelled back then mumbled something.

Richard looked at his phone, he slept right up until his alarm clock, the problem was, he felt even more tired than before. He caught a whiff of body odor and realized it was days since he had showered and brushed his teeth. The shower felt good to him, the hot water, the smell of the soap. He felt like himself again as he washed his pits and the back of his neck. He got out and loaded up the toothbrush with toothpaste and started brushing. He spit the toothpaste out and it was nothing but blood again. Then, another tooth simply fell out, it bounced around the sink a few times then went down the drain.

"I told you, you ain't getting rid of me," a voice inside Richard's head said. Richard looked up at the broken mirror and for a second his eyes were grey. They went back to normal and Richard spit some more and rinsed the blood out of the sink, then watched it swirl down the drain.

Richard then woke up again, he had a nightmare inside of a nightmare. He looked at the time and it was about time for him to get up.  He got up, took shower, lathered up and washed off.  He got out and put toothpaste on his toothbrush and hesitated for a second.  He then started brushing, no tooth fell out this time, nor was there any blood when he spit.

"You ain't got shit old man!" Richard said and laughed to himself.

He got dressed, prayed again, then biked to work, he was sore from the trek earlier but he still made good time.  He skipped the gas station, even though he was still tired and he grabbed the cigarettes out of his pocket, which he didn't remember putting them in his fresh uniform, while he was bike riding and crumbled up what was left, then tossed them down in the grass as he pulled into work.  He put his bike up with a smile on his face.  He was early and wanted to talk to Mr. Latrell.  He passed up Ron on his way to Mr. Latrell's room.

He looked at his watch, "Am I late?"

"No, I came in early to talk to Mr. Latrell, is he still up?"

"Yeah as far as I know," Ron said.

Richard nodded and walked down to Mr. Latrell's room and knocked on the door.

"Come in," Mr. Latrell said, from his recliner.

Richard opened the door, "Mr. Latrell, it's Richard from night shift, can I talk to you for a second?"

Mr. Latrell sat up, wonderment overcame his face, "Sure, what can I do for you?"

"You seem to be doing better tonight than the other night, so I just wanted to see if you could say a prayer for me."

"Well somedays I'm fine, somedays I'm not, but I haven't prayed, or at least I don't think I have, in a long time."

Richard walked up to Mr. Latrell, "If you want to grab a chair out of my kitchen and bring it in, I'll pray for you."

Richard done as he was told and set next to Mr. Latrell, "What am I praying for today?"

"I've been being haunted, I feel like a demon is trying to possess me," Richard said.

"A demon?" A weird smile formed on Mr. Latrell's face, "Has this demon told you its name by chance?"

"Yes, it's Jim."

Mr. Latrell broke out in laughter, he even covered his mouth to stop himself.

"What's so funny?" Richard asked, confused.

"A demon isn't going to have a simple name like that, a ghost maybe, but not a demon," he said, "I will still pray for you, so here take my hands," Mr. Latrell put his hands out and Richard took them. Mr. Latrell spoke in Latin again. Richard felt a great ease come over him. He reached for his St. Christopher and grasped it.  Mr. Latrell finished his prayer, then looked at Richard.

"I'm sorry, who are you?" he asked.

Richard was confused, "Its Richard from nightshift, you just prayed for me,"

Mr. Latrell's contorted, "Don't be stupid boy, prayer doesn't work. Now get out of my room!" Mr. Latrell's Alzheimer's came rearing its ugly head.

"I'm...umm..what?"

"I SAID GET OUT OF MY ROOM!" Mr. Latrell screamed.

Richard shot back and almost fell out of seat, he stood up and raced towards the door. He looked back at Mr. Latrell, "You crazy old shit!" he said and walked out.

He could still hear Mr. Latrell yelling as he walked up to his office, he caught Ron coming out of his office. He followed Ron up and let him out without saying much to him.

He made his first pot and took a sip, he savored the flavor, before swallowing. He then he headed up to the dining room.  He shut the curtains and turned around to see Leola behind the nurse's station, staring at him.  He walked by and nodded, then went and locked the garden doors.  He stopped by where the old door to the incinerator room was and stared at it.  He stared at it for a minute, waiting for blood, black ooze, or something to come spilling out of it, but it never did. The praying must have been helping ward of Jingling Jim.

He went and made a round, double checking his locks.  He checked the lobby floor and decided it was just going to get a scrubbing that night.  He went back down and got his coffee, he was expecting it to be cold, but it was warm. It appeared Jingling Jim was leaving Richard alone,  Richard just needed a little bit of faith.

Richard went and moved the tables, broke out the scrubber and put a polish to the floor.  He put the tables back out and put the chairs all around them.  He dumped the scrubber and looked where he had knocked a hole in the wall earlier.  He was wondering if he was just hallucinating everything from lack of sleep.  It didn't explain his first night but it explained the rest.

He went up to the lobby, moved the furniture to one side, scrubbed it, then moved the furniture to the other side.  He could not believe how well his night was going.  He emptied the scrubber for the second time and when he came out of the room, Leola was waiting for him.

She was wearing light blue, scrubs and had her hair done in pigtails, "Hey, how's it going?"

"Not too bad what's up?" Richard asked.

"Mrs. Faulson is having toilette issues, I tried but she has a cheap plunger," Leola said.

"Oh man! I could try the plunger in the janitor's closet," Richard said, "What room is she in?"

"W-Nineteen be warned it's bad," Leola said, pinched her nose, and waved her other hand in front of her face.

"Man, that sucks," Richard said.

Richard went and grabbed the plunger and headed to W-Nineteen, he knocked on the door, but got no response. He used his keys and opened the door. He went in slowly and announced himself, "Hello, it's Richard from security, I'm here to plunge your toilette."

"Ohhh, come in honey!" he heard a voice say from the middle room.

Richard walked in a little further and the smell hit him. It smelled of raw gas, a half-dead, rotted corpse and warm mayonnaise. Richard gagged and brought his hand up to his mouth. He didn't want to go in any further, but he had to.

"I think I had too much fiber in my diet," said Mrs. Faulson as she appeared from her bedroom and scared Richard a little bit, "I'm sorry honey, it's in my bedroom bathroom."

Mrs. Faulson looked like she was only in her forties and way too young to be in there. She had shoulder length black hair, with extraordinarily little grey eyes, she wore big-framed red glasses. She had crows' feet on around her eyes and a little bit of sagging skin under her neck. Her jawline was broad at first and narrowed to a slightly rounded chin. When she smiled, she had a moderate curve of youth to her smile.

"That's okay!" Richard said and went into the bedroom bathroom. His eyes were stinging from the stench, and he fought back the urge to vomit, making an audible gagging sound. He flipped the light on, to the bathroom and the only thing he could focus on was the toilette. It was filled to the brim with brown water, peas, carrots, corn all around a big, ball of feces.

He took the plunger and pushed down, a disgusting, wet, squishing and suctioning noise was heard as he pushed down through the feces.  He repeated the process six more times, the squishing sound got less and less, but the water got more and more brown.  Finally, after about fifteen minutes of plunging, he heard a noise of suction that let him know he had pushed the mass through.  He lifted the plunger out and pushed the handle on the tank.  The feces stew swirled around then went down the drain.  Richard snagged an empty trash bag and wrapped his plunger in it.

"Thank you! I think I'll spray some perfume to cover up that smell," Mrs. Faulson laughed.

"Let's hope it works," Richard joked back.

He left the room, then took the plunger to the cleaning room and sprayed it down.  He tossed the bag in the trash cart and looked at the time.  He needed to do his first trash run of the night, but washed his hands first.

He grabbed the grey cart and hit the west hall trash room.  It was filled up that night, but Richard didn't mind, he loaded up the trash and when he pulled the cart back out, Leola was there and Richard jumped.

"I owe you lunch for unclogging that toilette," she said and smiled.

"I don't think I want lunch after unclogging that toilette," Richard laughed.

"I don't blame you, it smelled like she had shit out straight death."

"She's rotten from inside," Richard said, "I'm going to get this trash going, I'll talk at you when I get done."

"Okay!"

Richard went down to east hall and loaded up more trash, he went up and dumped it, because he believed he wouldn't have had enough room to load up the kitchen trash.  While he was compacting, he looked at the cigarette burns from the cigarettes he flipped at it. He shook his head and headed down to the kitchen.

He stopped when walked into the dock area where the trashcans were.  Nothing was put in the trashcans except the grease. There  were three big piles of food waste and cardboard, just sitting on the floor.  Richard's blood began to boil, he walked over and kicked the grease can over then walked out of there, he wasn't touching that trash and planned on staying over in the morning to confront the staff.

He went to his bathroom in his office and washed his hands, then heated up the last cup of coffee, from the first pot of coffee. He sat down and reviewed some cameras, and watched the one on the dock.  He could clearly see himself kicking the grease can over, so he was positive he was going to get in trouble, but he could also see the piles of trash on the floor.

"You'll be alright, it's justified, I'm sure Sheila will understand," Richard said to himself.

Then, before he knew it, it was time to let in first shift.  He went up and unlocked the door and this time there was someone else there.  He looked almost like an off-season Santa Claus.  He had on grey scrubs and red lanyard with his name badge on it, which read, "Brad"

Richard opened the doors and asked, "Where's Doug?"

"He quit!" Brad said, his voice somewhat feminine, "I'm Brad by the way," he said walked in.  He had a girlish sway to his walk and Richard questioned in his head that Brad might be gay.

"Brad, I'm Richard the night security. What did he quit for?"

Brad chuckled, "He said the night security guy creeped him out."

"Now that's funny!' Richard laughed and led Brad to the elevator.

"I have to get used to the warm weather here," Brad said as they boarded the elevator, sweat already forming on his brow.

"Where you from?"

"Me and my husband are from upper Michigan, we moved here because he got a job opportunity. I didn't want to I hate anything warmer than sixty-five degrees," Brad said.

"Well, if you don't like the weather here in Indiana, it'll change five minutes later," Richard said and Brad laughed.

The elevator opened and Richard pointed to the nurse's station, "That's where you need to be headed," Richard said and then headed back into his office.

Half an hour later there came Mark a knocking, "Hey, how'd it go?" he asked.

"W-Nineteen had a clog, but I got it. I have a question for you though. What time does the kitchen staff come in? They left one hell of mess and I refuse to clean it up."

"Tim, usually a little after you leave, he's the manager. You gonna say something to him? He's kind of an ass."

"Yeah, I am it's kind of bullshit because I didn't put a liner in the trash can."

"That sounds petty as hell. If you're staying over, I'll knock on your door when I see him."

"Thank you!" Richard said.

Richard clocked out and waited in the office for the knock on the door. It came about thirty minutes later, and Richard was more than happy to answer the door.

"Tim is headed into his office," Mark said.

"I plan to as well."

Richard headed down to the end of east hall and saw a glimpse of Tim. He was rather tall, with a large, rounded head, and a crewcut. He had wide shoulders that shifted when he walked. He was wearing a light pink and blue, plaid, long-sleeved shirt and light brown pants. He rounded the corner and Richard walked faster to catch up to him.

As Richard rounded the corner, he heard Tim yell out in anger, "WHAT THE HELL IS THIS?" Then he heard stuff getting knocked over and tossed about. Richard prepared himself for confrontation as he walked through the set of double doors that led into the kitchen.

Tim was coming from the dock doors and stopped when he saw Richard, "Are you the night janitor?"

"No, I'm security, what's the problem?" Richard asked.

"Security my ass, you're a glorified janitor. Why didn't you pick up the trash?" he brought his finger up and pointed at Richard.

"Why was it not put in the trash can, it was dumped on the floor. It's not my job to pick up after your lazy ass!" Richard said and raised his voice.

"There wasn't a liner in the trash can," Tim said as his cheeks reddened.

"Big fregging deal, you can't put a liner in a trashcan? My job says to empty the trashcans, which I do, doesn't say anything about replacing them," Richard said and took a step closer to Tim.

"You take another step and I'll drop you!" Tim stepped up towards Richard and puffed his chest up.

"Do it, I dare you. I'm not intimidated by you, just because you're bigger than me. I will drop you and just imagine when everyone finds out that a little old me, dropped a big, hulking man like you."

There was silence for a minute, Richard could tell Tim wasn't used to be talked back to, then Tim spoke, "Get out of my kitchen!"

Richard turned around and started walking out, "Pick your shit up, because I won't do it tonight either and when this place gets roaches because of your lazy ass, I'm sure they send you sailing right on out of here," Richard said and flipped Tim off as he walked away.

Richard thought for a minute he was going to lose his cool, but he was happy that kept his composure.  He didn't say anything to Mark on the way out, just left.  The bike ride felt so much better that morning.

There wasn't breakfast waiting for him this time around. So he took a shower and some sleeping pills and waited for them to kick in.

What Richard didn't know, was he didn't get rid of Jingling Jim, Jingling Jim got rid of him.  He didn't have enough energy to keep possessing Richard's body and the praying didn't help, prayer never helps.  He needed fear and Richard wasn't doing much to cause fear.  Him and Richard killed a few people, but there wasn't enough fear from those deaths. Jingling Jim was going to have to go back to his old ways of haunting and eating the souls of the ones he haunted.  It was going to take him longer to get back into Richards body, but one way or another, he was going to do it.

Richard woke up at the sound of his alarm, he had no dreams that day. He took another shower, got dressed and once again, his mom wasn't around, but there was food on the table.  She had made homemade tamales and left him some for work, it was Bingo night and she was feeling lucky.  Richard smiled, he was feeling great.

He stopped off at the gas station and grabbed a can of coffee. On his way to work, he got to thinking about the past two weeks' events, he was stressed out, tired, and looked too much into the backstory of The Gardens. He had psychologically sabotaged himself. Richard didn't have any recollections of the murders, just blank spots in his memories, so he didn't feel any remorse.  How could he have any remorse, if he had no memory of them?

Ron was sitting down in the lobby when Richard approached the doors.  Ron saw Richard at the door and raced up to the doors and opened them, "Sorry man, was resting a few and lost track of time."

"No worries, rough night?"

"Well, football was on and the cable went out, then they fixed it, all the T.V.s needed reset, then they wouldn't reset.  I had to call them out and get this, they wanted me to read the numbers off every cable box here in the building.”

“What did you tell them?” Richard asked as they got on the elevator.

“I told them hell no, I don’t get paid to do their job, they sent two people out at eight and they got done right before you showed up. Other than that, not a bad night.”

“Good!”

“I heard you put Tim in his place.”

“Well, I tried, I’ll find out if he got the message.”

“According to Mark he went to Sheila and James over it, they told him to do his job and shut up, not in those words, but close.”

The elevator opened and Richard could see Leola up at the nurse’s station.  She was talking to Michelle and a few other people who Richard assumed were other CNA’s.  He smiled at her and went into his office and there sitting on his desk, was a note.  It was from Sheila, she wanted to see him in the morning and talk about what happened with Tim.

“Great!,” Richard said and crumbled up the note and threw it away.  He put his lunch in the fridge and opened the coffee.  He took a big whiff of it and let the nutty flavor hit his nose.  He took the scoop out of the other coffee can and scooped out a few scoops into the coffee maker.  He got the water, poured it in and turned on his happiness.  He poured himself a cup and waited for the knock on the door from Ron.  The knock came a short time after.  He walked Ron up with his coffee cup in hand and didn’t spill a drop.

He sat the cup down on the receptionist desk, locked the doors and then picked it back up. He was once again in good mood as he headed back down to his office.  He drank his cup, rinsed it out and put it up, then headed up to the dining room and shut the curtains.  He went and locked the garden doors, but not before he made a round inside, he rather enjoyed the garden area, it was a shame he only got to see it temporarily.

He was walking down west hall when a resident on east hall stuck their head out the door and waved for at Richard.  Richard waved back and headed towards the resident. As he approached, he could see a look of frustration on the wrinkled face of the resident.

The resident was tall but slouched over, he had grey hair on the sides of his head and none on top.  His once brown eyes were filmed over with glaucoma. He had on red and green flannel pajamas and had a slight wobble to him.

"What seems to be the problem?" Richard asked.

"Well, I set my DVR to record the football game because I was gone most of the day, but the only thing it recorded was the cable company logo," the resident said.  Richard looked at the black and white nametag on the door so he could properly address the resident.

"Mr. Belvidair, I don't think there would be much I can do. The cable was out so that's what got recorded."

"NO! it should have recorded the game, I know how this works." Mr. Belvidair said, his demeanor quickly changing.

"It can't record, if there isn't anything to record Mr. Belvidair," Richard said.

Mr. Belvidair raised his hand above his head and clenched his fist, "ARE YOU CALLING ME STUPID!" he yelled.

Richard stepped back and the yell caught the attention of Michelle.  She came out of the nurse's station in a hurry an came down the hall to rescue Richard before Mr. Belvidair got violent.

"You put that hand down Mr. Belvidair, I have permission from your doctor to give you forty-c.c.'s of Ativan if you get out of hand," Michelle said and walked in between Mr. Belvidair and Richard.

"Well I can't watch my game," he said to her and lowered his hand.

"No one could, the cable went out, not that you could see it anyways glaucoma eyes!" she harped.

"Bitch!" Mr. Belvidair said, went in his room and slammed the door.

"Wow, thank you for that!" Richard said.

"Not an issue, he's on his way out soon, money issues," Michelle said.

"Good, with anger like that it'd be a matter of time before he hurt someone," Richard said and shook his head.

Richard turned around and went back up east hall, and headed to his office. He looked back and Leola was coming out from behind the nurse's station, tears streaked her cheeks. She rushed by Richard and went to the women's bathroom. Richard continued making his way to his office, he poured him a cup of coffee and heated it up in the microwave. He sat down and reviewed the cameras when there came a knock on the door. When he opened it, it was Leola, still visibly shaken.

"What's up?" Richard asked.

"Can I get up cup of coffee, like regular coffee?" she asked and held out a pink cup, "and can we talk for a second?"

"Yea sure," Richard said and poured her a cup, and put it in the microwave for her. They remained in silence the whole time the coffee heated up, but once she took a sip of the coffee, she started talking.

"My boyfriend broke up with me tonight," she said and took another sip of coffee.

"Wow, why? Richard asked.

"He said my night shift was interfering with our personal life."

"That's silly!"

"I know, I got to go to school in the evenings and work at nights, we have the weekends together."

"Well, it's his loss, I don't know you very well, but I think you're a nice person."

"Well thank you! Sorry to unload on you, just couldn't believe it, he broke up with me over text messaging."

"Don't apologize, anytime you need to talk, you know where my office is."

Leola finished her coffee and left Richard's office with a smile on her face.  She went behind the nurse's station and looked at her messages again, she shook her head, she put her phone away and went and done a room check on the residents that needed it.

After Mr. Belvidair's fit, he went and sat down in his recliner and picked up his remote, "Damned bunch of idiots around here," he said as he pressed the buttons on the remote, nothing happened at first, then his T.V. went all staticky, he then hit the remote and a picture appeared.

The image was of a black and white Jingling Jim holding a football on a football field, but Mr. Belvidair didn't know who that was.  To Mr. Belvidair it was just some scrawny, homely, toothless, looking man on his screen, holding a football.  Jingling Jim was standing on the fifty-yard line of the football field.  The picture was slightly grainy and Jingling Jim took a pose of a quarterback getting ready to receive the ball from the center lineman.

"DOOOOOWNNN! SEEEEEEEEEET! HUT! HUT! HUT!" Jingling Jim ran backwards with the ball.  He brought his arm back as if he were going to throw it.

"What the hell is he doing, that idiot, there's no one on the field!" Mr. Belvidair said and stood up.

Jingling Jim winked and threw the football.  It came out of the T.V. and hit Mr. Belvidair square in the nose.  He grabbed his nose and screamed out.   He fell backwards into his recliner, and the recliner tipped back and over. Mr. Belvidair was sure his nose was broken, but it wasn't, there was no blood, no pain, and no football anywhere in sight when he opened his eyes.

With his feet in the air and looking at the ceiling, Mr. Belvidair had to roll himself over to the side of the recliner.  He then struggled to get up, knocking over his nightstand as he done so.  After a few minutes he was able to stand with the help of pushing up on his couch to steady him.  He took and rocked the recliner back and forth a few times before he was able to get it right side up.  He then turned to look back at the T.V.

"BOOOOO!" Jingling Jim said and scared Mr. Belvidair so badly that he fell, once again, into the recliner.  Mr. Belvidair grabbed his chest as it tightened up, he struggled to breathe, his heart pounded irregularly.  Jingling Jim's face had a twisted smile on his face, "That's right....feeeeaarrrr meee," he whispered as he placed his hand above Mr. Belvidair's chest, "feeeeeaaarrrr meeeeee!" he said as he plunged his ghostly hand into Mr. Belvidair's chest and wrapped his lengthy fingers around Mr. Belvidair's heart and slowly began to squeeze.   Mr. Belvidair's eyes grew wide. Jingling Jim opened his mouth as a white haze formed over Mr. Belvidair, it was his fear and Jingling Jim was going to feast on it.  Jingling Jim drew in a breath and sucked in Mr. Belvidair's fear.   After a few breaths in, Mr. Belvidair was no more.

Richard got up after he finished his cup of coffee and headed to the dining room.  The floor still looked nice and shiny, so he decided once again, that it would only need to be scrubbed.  He put up all the tables and chairs, then scrubbed the floor.  He noticed the small hole he had put in the wall was still there and smiled at the thought, that he hadn't been blamed for it yet.

He worked a little faster that night scrubbing the floors because he remembered he needed to do some carpet extraction.

He went up and down the halls to see if they even needed it and used better judgement to say they didn't need it, "Man, I can't believe I forgot to scrub carpets this week," he said to himself.

"Well, I think they look fine!" he heard Leola say behind him.

"Yeah, I was supposed to do them Tuesday I think and I scrubbed floors instead. On top of that I have to see Sheila in the morning over and incident with Tim," Richard said, as his anxiety picked up.

"I think everything will be okay," Leola smiled at him.

"I hope so, I need this job," Richard looked at his watch, "Well, I have to do my trash run, I hope the trash wasn't like it was last night."

"Well, get with me after your trash haul, I sure could use another cup of coffee," she smiled again.

"Will do," Richard said and went and got his cart.  The trash was a little fuller than the night before in the west hall and just about as full on the east hall.  Richard was going to have to make two trips.

He took his first load to the compactor.  The air was muggy, it was little hard for Richard to breathe.  He was sweating before he even unloaded the trash. Even the slight breeze that blew was warm and sticky.  The compactor seemed to work harder that night, straining a little as it crushed.

Richard was focusing on the sky, trying to drown out the sickly, sounding compactor when he caught something out of the corner of his eye.  He thought maybe Leola followed him out but, when he looked, no one was there.  His mind and heart starting racing, he started asking himself in his head, "What if it that was Jingling Jim?". He could feel his heart racing in his chest as he raced back inside with the cart and headed to the kitchen.  He completely passed Leola in the hall, who said something to him, but he didn't hear because of the beating drum of a heartbeat in his ears.

He went down into the kitchen and out to the dock and stopped dead in his tracks.  All the trash was picked up, but instead of two trashcans and the grease bucket, there were four trashcans. They had liners in them, but they were packed to the brim with trash and food products. Some of the stuff on top looked as if it had been plunged from a drain and set there on purpose.  It smelled like it had come from a drain as well.  There was another note for him.

"These barrels are to be cleaned tonight and ready for me in the morning-TIM." To make matters worse there was a smiley face next to Tim's name.

Richard kept the note this time and took pictures of the trashcans before he dumped them.  It took everything he had to lift the bags out of the cans, not to mention fighting the urge to vomit from the smell.  He hoisted the last bag in and let out a small grunt as he done so.  He was dreading loading it into the crash compactor and the mere thought of seeing Jingling Jim, sent chills down his spine.  He was still hoping Jingling Jim was just a figment from stress.

He took the trash back down east hall and Leola stopped about ten feet away from him, "Lord that stinks!" she said and pinched her nose.

"Yeah, another present from Tim, now I can't wait to talk to Sheila. I kept the note and took pictures this time, I really hate that guy!"

"I'm going to run out to Taco House here in a few, you want anything?"

"Nah, I'm good, I got homemade tamales, plus my mom will probably have breakfast waiting for me."

"You still live with your mom?" Leola asked and giggled like the thought was surreal.

"Yes, pretty much grew up without a dad, so I owe it to her to help her out now, nothing wrong with that," Richard said offended at Leola's attitude.

"I didn't mean anything by it, I just…" she went to go say but Richard interrupted her.

"No, it's all cool, learning the whole story is always crucial. I got to get this out before this stinks up the whole building," Richard said and shook his head as he went by.

Once out to the compactor, Richard's heart started racing again. He thought he heard someone walking up behind him but there wasn't anyone behind him when he turned around. Jingling Jim was doing exactly what he set out to do, cause fear so he can go back to taking over Richard's body. Richard focused on the sky again, it was slightly cloudy, which only trapped the warm air in. The compactor rumbled and moaned again as it crushed the trash.

He walked back inside, took the trash cart to the cleaning room and sprayed it out. He avoided Leola for the rest of the night. He was expecting her to come knocking for some coffee but she never did and Richard was kind of glad, he didn't want to be bothered. He made another round, checking the doors again, to make sure they weren't tampered with, then headed in and even though it was hot outside, wanted more coffee. He stayed in his office until it was time to let Brad in.

"Hello there!" Brad said as he walked flamboyantly in and smiled at Richard.

"Hello!" is all Richard said as they walked to the elevator. It was a quiet ride down as Richard got to thinking about Sheila coming in.

He went back to his office, cleaned out the coffee pot, rinsed his face off because he felt sticky from the heat still, then waited for Mark to come knocking on his door. The knock came about twenty minutes later and he didn't want to answer it at first, but he did.

"How'd it go tonight?" Mark asked, wrinkled his brow and adjusted his hat.

"A little odd to say the least…" was all Richard could say before a scream broke out down the hall.

Richard and Mark took off up the ramp towards the sound of the scream and when they rounded the east hall corner, Leola ran out of a room, right into the arms of Richard, "What's going on?'

"Mr. Belividair is dead!" she said.

"What's wrong with you, ain't ever seen a dead body before?" Mark asked rudely.

"NO!" Leola and pulled away from Richard as if he said it.

"You're in the wrong profession then," Mark said and huffed.

Leola just walked away and Mark huffed something under his breath as Richard looked at his watch, it was almost seven. The dayshift nurse told Michelle she would handle it and to go home. Richard and Michelle rode up in the elevator together with Leola nowhere in sight.

"You have a good day!" Michelle said as she left.

"You as well," Richard said and noticed he hadn't seen Tim walk by.

The sun was shining bright when a lady walked through the door. She was of medium height, skinny, brunette and wore her hair in a braided ponytail. She had soft, brown eyes and smiled at Richard. She wore a red dress and matching heels.

"Hi, I'm Brittany!" she said and walked by Richard.

"I'm Richard, I'm waiting on Sheila, she said she needed to talk to me this morning."

"Oh! She was pulling in as I was getting out, in fact," she looked out the glass doors, "Here she comes now."

Richard looked up and walking towards the sliding, glass doors was Sheila. She was wearing a blue t-shirt, with "The Gardens" on it, tight fit blue jeans, with brown shoes. She had her shoulder length, blonde hair, clipped with pink barrettes on the side.  She smiled as she walked in.

"I'm here to talk about Tim," Richard said.

"Yes, I'm sorry to keep you over, but gotten many complaints against him. So, what he said about you, I've taken with a grain of salt, I need your side of the story," she said and motioned for him to come behind the receptionist desk where Brittany was sitting. Richard followed and went into her office with her.

She got behind her desk and sat down, "Have a seat and tell me your side."

Richard sat down in the black, soft comfortable chair. It was like the chair was made for him, the arm rests were at the perfect height, "Well, I got a note from Tim that I needed to put liners back in my trashcans, which I'm sorry I don't carry trash bags with me and there isn't any in the trashcans.  He's not my boss, he doesn't need to be telling me what to do.  So, I don't put liners in them and I come in the next night and there is garbage all over floor and they keep filling up the grease can to where I can hardly move it. So, last night I go in there and there's another note, I saved that one," Richard said and handed it to Sheila, "and he added trash cans and filled them to the brim," Richard showed her the pictures, "I don't know what this guy's problem is, but it's annoying."

"Tim said you confronted him, got verbally aggressive and flipped him off?" Sheila asked with a smile.

"That I did, I won't lie to you, he made me mad. Now he wants me to clean his barrels, that's not my job."

"Well, I'm marking down you denied the flipping off, since there's no proof, and I really don't like him, he can't prove it. Otherwise you'll get in trouble," Sheila laughed and scribbled somethings down, "Can you send me those pictures? You have my email right?"

"Yes that's right!"

"Send me those as soon as you can please!"

Richard pulled up his email on his phone, typed in Sheila's address, attached the photos, and sent them, "There ya go, you should have them," Richard said, then heard a ding come from Sheila's computer.

Richard watched as her blue eyes searched the screen and she clicked on a few things, "Wow, what an ass!" she said.

"Yep!" Richard said and sighed.

"Well, you can go, I got all I need from you and hopefully Tim won't be here too much longer." Sheila smiled from behind the computer screen.

"You have a nice day!" Richard said and got up to leave.

"You too, go home and get some rest."

"I plan to."

After than Richard left and rode home. The weather was hot though, so a shower was going to be in order.  He had another great breakfast waiting for him. He wolfed it down, did the dishes, took some pills then went to bed.

From the time Officer Thompson got off the phone with Richard to Saturday, when he decided to stake out Mr. Helsir's house, all he done was think about Mr. Helsir. There was something about him that was addicting. He found his house on the southern edge of town and was slightly disappointed in its size. He figured with as much money Mr. Helsir had, he would have a larger house.

The house was a brick, ranch-style house. The lawn needed mowed and the bushes that lined the driveway and front of the house were all overgrown. The driveway's asphalt was all cracked and he didn't see a car in the driveway. There was a shutter missing on the far, left window and a few panes were cracked on two of the three windows that lined the front.

Officer Thompson checked the address again and looked through a pair of binoculars from down the road. He wanted to get a closer look and being he was doing a stake out, he wore grey sweatpants and grey sweatshirt that had the sleeves cut off and a hood. He spied a big, black mailbox by the road in front of the house and could see the door wasn't shut, because of overflowing mail.

He put his binoculars up and got out of the car. He pretended to be a jogger and jogged towards the mailbox. He stopped and pretended to tie his shoe, while leaning over to tie his shoe, and swiped a piece of mail as he done so and stuffed it in the front pocket of his hoodie. He then jogged down the road, turned around and jogged back to his car and got in.

He pulled the crumpled up, piece of mail from his pocket and looked at the address, "Johnathan Helsir, 2020 West Jefferson, Yertzville, Indiana 46123". He didn't bother opening it, he had the proof he needed that it was Mr. Helsir's house. He sat back and waited a few more hours to see if a car pulled in or out.

He had to use the bathroom while waiting but didn't want to drive away. He looked around, the sun was still bright and even though the only house on the road, he was skeptical about using the bathroom in his car. Finally, after another thirty minutes he had that dull pain in his bladder that told him, it was now or never. He grabbed an empty water bottle, hurriedly pulled his pants down, aimed the best he could and relieved himself in the water bottle. "It's all part of the job," he said as he filled the water bottle, stopped, dumped out what he had and started to urinate again in the bottle. After the second fill, he was done, he emptied the bottle again in the street and watched the house once more.

The sun had set and Officer Thompson was eating a bologna sandwich when he decided to make a move. He crumpled up the saranwrap and tossed it into the back of his seat. He wiped mayo off his lip with his thumb and got out of his car. There wasn't even a streetlight around, he was completely in the dark. He opted out of using his flashlight, and walked slowly up the driveway, and up next to the house. He tried looking through the window but curtains blocked his view. He was positive there was no one there, so he tried the door handle it was locked.

He decided to try the back door, even though there wasn't anyone else around, he wanted to play it safe. He made his way around back, crouched down, with his back against the house. There was no gate to go through, not protected whatsoever, so it was rather easy to make it around to the back door. It too was locked, but Officer Thompson was proficient at picking locks and always carried a kit with him in his wallet.

He took a small, thin, metal piece with a curved end and put it in the lock, curved end down. He then took another, thin piece of metal that was about two inches long, and had a few curves to it. He slid the curvy piece onto the first piece and wiggled it up and down as he worked it until it stopped moving. He had a final, thicker piece, that wasn't as long as the other one and slid it on top of the curvy piece. He worked them around a few more times, then the lock twisted up and he was able to open the door, slowly.

He tried a light switch, to the right of the door, but there was no electricity.  He then used his phone's flashlight function, to start to look around. He was standing in a kitchen, there was a table and chairs but no sign it had ever been used, nothing was on the table. He moved his phone around and there were cabinets and a sink to the left of him.  There was no soap on the sink and when he looked in the cabinets, there were no dishes.  He turned around and there was a fridge, but he didn't bother opening it because if there was no electricity, there was probably nothing in the it.

Where the table was at, led into the living room. There was an old couch that had cabins printed on it with dark, walnut legs.  A pale blue recliner covered in dust and a brass lamp and dusty lampshade.  There was a hallway at the far left of the living room, he cautiously walked down it.  There was a door to his right he opened it and it was room, with blue, shag carpet and an old bed with a flower printed mattress, that hadn't been laid on in years.  He walked further down the hall and went to another door and opened it.  It was a bathroom with lime-green tile, toilet and shower.  There were two more doors down the hall, one to the right and one at the end of the hall.  Both were rooms with the same, disgusting carpet, but no furniture.

He walked in the main bedroom, there was a bathroom straight back from the door.  Officer Thompson proceeded with caution as he walked further into the room.  There was a closet with a slotted door, to the right of the bathroom door and for a second, he thought he saw something reflective.  He stopped and reached down to retrieve the 38 special he always kept strapped to his ankle.

"This is Officer Thompson with the Yertzville P.D., come out of the closet, slowly!" he said and pointed his gun towards the closet. There was silence, then he heard his heart beating in his ears.  He didn't realize he was holding his breath and let out a rather loud sigh. Then he took a few more steps towards the closet.  He slowly reached out and put his hand on the knob of the closet, it felt dirty under his fingers.  He took a deep breath in and yanked the door open. He let his breath out as he realized the reflection of light was coming from a metal rod   He sighed and shook his head, he turned around and all went dark.

When Officer Thompson woke up, his head was pounding, his vision was blurred and the back of his neck felt wet and sticky. He was in a sitting position, and there was something in his mouth, it felt fuzzy on his tongue and was preventing him from closing his mouth.  There was a single light hanging above, but away from him. He could hear water trickling from somewhere around him.  He couldn't see but three feet in front of him.  His hands were tied behind his back and tried to wiggle free, but he couldn't and his feet were tied to the legs of the chair.

"Welcome, Officer Thompson, it's a shame we have to meet this way," a soft, southern voice said, from behind him.  Officer Thompson felt someone playing with the knot on his gag and then it came loose.

"Who are you?" Officer Thompson asked.

"Well if you're here, you already know who I am.  The question is, why are you looking for Mr. Helsir?" Mr. Helsir asked.

"You just referred to yourself in the third person," Officer Thompson pointed out.

"That I did, but I still ask, why?"

"Mr. Helsir only existed about five years ago, but he didn't exist before that. You know who did though? Johnathon McCurdy, but he disappeared and you popped up.  I think it's really ironic, that you bought the very place that Johnathon McCurdy's father burnt down." Officer Thompson spewed out, "Does Jingling Jim McCurdy sound familiar to you."

There was dead silence for a minute then Mr. Helsir started clapping, "Great detective skills, odd how such a small-town cop figured it out, but the government did not.  They should promote you...well they won't be able to after tonight.  I can't let you ruin this for me."

"Ruin what?"

"I've waited and waited for the man who stopped my dad, son to grow up. I made sure I got the building his dad destroyed my dad in. I made sure he got fired from his other job and I made sure he got hired at The Gardens. Unlike his father, I don't think Richard will make it out alive."

"I found my father's body still in the incinerator, they never gave him a proper burial, so his spirit could rest. I made a deal with the devil so to speak and summoned his spirit back to The Gardens. I wasn't expecting it to take this long, but I'm sure my dad knows what he is doing." Johnathon laughed.

"You're a psycho, you actually think your dad's spirit still lives on and is haunting The Gardens. You went through all this trouble, for a ghost?" Officer Thompson asked and laughed, "I guess that's about as smart as starting a fire in a building while you're still in it. I guess the apple doesn't fall far from the tree."

The gag was put back in Officer Thompson's mouth. Johnathon walked in front of Officer Thompson, he was wearing a black suit, with a red tie and nice, shiny, black shoes. He had short, black hair with a fade haircut. He had thins lips and half smile on his face, and even though it was dark in the room he had sunglasses on. He had a hammer in one hand and a long, flathead screwdriver in the other. He looked just like his father, but with more teeth and less beard. His eyes matched his father's exactly, cold, piercing, and unforgiving.

"I'm going to enjoy tearing you apart!" Johnathon said and brought the screwdriver up to the front tooth of Officer Thompson, that was hanging over the gag. Officer Thompson started to thrash about, "I wouldn't do that if I were you, I might miss and end this sooner than later."

Johnathon took the hammer and hit the screwdriver on the butt of the handle, knocking Officer Thompson's front tooth out. Officer Thompson screamed, but with the gag, it was muffled.

Johnathon went to the next tooth and the next tooth.  He took out about eight teeth before stopping.  He then knelt and removed Officer Thompson's shoes and socks.  He then placed the flathead right by the cuticle on the big toe, at an angle, then struck.  That was it for Officer Thompson, the pain was too much and he passed out.

Johnathon wasn't done with Officer Thompson, he was going to make a statement out of him.  He untied Officer Thompson and laid him face down on the cold, concrete floor.  He then went back to a table that housed all his special tools.  He had a set tools, that he kept wrapped in human skin that was about three feet long and foot wide, rolled up.  He untied the thin piece of human skin that kept the wrap tied.  He unrolled it and ran his lengthy fingers over the knives, saws and shears.

The set was well taken care of, it was found by Johnathon after his dad passed and according to his mom, belonged to his great grandpa from overseas, who moved to Chicago later in life. Once Johnathon got them, he cleaned them up and restored them, taking off any blood stains and rust that were on them.

He took out a scalpel, with a much curvier blade than a normal scalpel.  It was great for cutting down a spine because the blade didn't catch the bone but cut just above it.  He also used it to cut shirts off people, which is what he did.  He cut the shirt off Officer Thompson and exposed his back.  He then took the scalpel and started at the back of Officer Thompson's head and cut all the way down to his waistline.

He got up to get a set of shears when Officer Thompson started to scream out, "Oh no, we can't have that."  He grabbed the scalpel back up and knelt over Officer Thompson, he placed the blade in between each SCM muscle and poked it in, and slide it across, severing the voice box.  A whistly gasp filled the air and Johnathon smiled, "I love that sound."

Officer Thompson froze in fear, he couldn't move.  He couldn't move as his pants were cut off, or as Johnathon cut down to his tailbone, then put his fingers in the middle of his back and pulled the flesh from muscles.  Tears fell out of his eyes as Johnathon cut down the back of his arms and around his wrist.  He grew weak, and his eyes grew heavy, then he shut them from the last time.

Johnathon field dressed Officer Thompson like a deer.  He put Officer Thompson's flesh in a trash bag, tied his feet together then strung him upside down, Officer Thompson's fingertips gently swept the concrete floor, smearing what blood he had left that dripped from his body.

"I do believe I'll add this to my collection," Johnathon said and picked up the trash bag full of skin.

Johnathon carried the bag of skin, his folding table and tools up from the basement of the warehouse that he took Officer Thompson to.  He wasn't worried about leaving fingerprints because he didn't have any, he removed them with acid.  His hair was from multiple sources, that he had surgically plugged in his scalp.  He aslo had his scalp surgically removed and replaced with a skin graft so he had no natural hair on his head before adding in the fake hair. He had the rest of his body hair lasered off. If they found a hair, whose ever they found, would lead back to numerous missing people from around Indiana. He dialed 9-1-1 on Officer Thompson's phone, then tossed it into some bushes.  He loaded everything up in his 1979, blue metal flake, Cadillac and headed to his real house.

Richard was sound asleep when he heard his mom calling from the front room, "RICHARD! RICHARD COME HERE!"

Richard, groggily, got up and walked to the living room, where Maria was sitting in her recliner with a tray over her lap that had food on it, "Something happened to your friend!"

"What?" Richard said and yawned, then rubbed his eyes.

"Officer Thompson, watch!" she said and pointed to the television.

Richard looked over as the broadcast started, "We come to you tonight with the unbearable news of the loss of one of Yertzville's own, Officer Perry Thompson.  He was found in a sub-basement of a building in the abandoned industrial park, just outside of Yertzville.  Here is Cathy with the story," the news announcer said.

"Hi, this is Cathy Calhoun with WRTV one.  I come to you tonight with a horrible story and loss of one of our own.  Officer Perry Thompson called 9-1-1 this morning and his phone was found just beyond those bushes over there," the camera panned out to a set of bushes. "When ambulances arrived EMTs couldn't find Officer Thompson, so they called in the YPD. After a long search, they found a gruesome discovery in one of the sub-basements, in the warehouses over there.  Officer Thompson was found, field-dressed like a deer, hanging upside down.  I have with me, Sargent Rickers of the YPD.  What can you tell me so far."

The camera focused on Sargent Rickers.  Rickers was rather tall and round, he had two chins and the textbook mustache for police officers.  He wore aviator sunglasses that he took off aggressively and stared at the camera with his dark, brown eyes,

"Some sick son-of-a-bitch stole his skin….WHO THE HELL DOES THAT?" he yelled.

"Stole his skin?" Richard asked himself in shock.

"What exactly do you mean, they stole his skin?" Cathy asked Rickers.

Well, is pretty goddamned self-explanatory there princess, some sick bastard skinned him alive and took his skin."

The camera went over to Cathy's face and she was a little teary-eyed from Sargent Rickers's verbal attack, "I'm sorry, I just thought I missed something."

"Well, clean your ears," Sargent Rickers snapped and walked out of view of the camera.

"Well, this has been the worst thing to happen to Yertzville since the burning of The Gardens.  This is Cathy Calhoun and I will keep you informed on any new updates.  Have a goodnight, back to you Lennie."

Whatever else was said Richard blocked out.  He walked over to the couch and sat down, trying to process what he had just heard.  A sickly image of his friend's skinless body filled his head.

"Are you okay?" Maria asked.

"Yeah momma, I'll be okay just some shocking news. I'm..umm, I'm gonna head back to bed and try to lay down for a little bit." Richard said and got up, still in shock.

He walked back to his room, popped a few more sleeping pills and laid back down.  It was another thirty minutes before the pills kicked and Richard was sound asleep. It didn't take long before Richard was dreaming.

Richard's dream soon turned into nightmare. At first, he was standing in a well-lit room, then all of sudden all the lights went out. There was something creaking in the room he was in, but he couldn't see it.  The center of the room then took on a blue, moonlit appearance.  There was something swinging through the edge of the light, that was causing the creaking noise.  Richard couldn't tell what it was at first, so he got closer.

It swung through the light and into the darkness, Richard took another step.  It swung through again and he got closer.  It looked like a body hanging upside down, but it swung out of the light once more.  He stepped into the light, but the body never came back through into the light.

"What the hell?" Richard asked himself, then heard wet, slopping footsteps behind him.  He was afraid to turn around, but he slowly did.  When he did, there stood a skinned, bloody Officer Thompson.

"This is your fault!" he said, his eyelid-less eyes stared right at Richard.

"Mine, what do you mean?" Richard said as they started to circle each other.

"If you wouldn't have asked for my help, I wouldn't have gotten involved, now my wife is a widow and my kids are fatherless."

"You could have said no, I would have understood," Richard said, he couldn't take his eyes off Officer Thompson.

"I could have but I didn't, I did a favor for you and now you have to pay me back."

"What are you talking about? I'm not paying you back, you're dead."

"So was Jingling Jim and he came back, I sure would hate to come back and go after Maria, your dear mom."

"My momma has nothing to do with this!" Richard screamed.

"Neither did I, this was between you and Jingling Jim, you could have just let him take over, but you had to fight him. Now look, I'm dead as will your mom be."

"NOOOOOOOOOOO!" Richard screamed and then woke. He rushed out of bed and into the living room, where he found his mom, fast asleep.

Richard wiped the sweat from his brow, then went and took a shower. He kept it hot and the let steam relax him and fill the room. He leaned his head up against the wall and let the water run down the back of his neck and back, "This can't be happening again," he said himself, as the image of the skinned Officer Thompson danced in his head. He finally shook the image from his head and got out of the shower.

Steam had covered the broken mirror and Richard looked it, "I need to get this fixed," he said and carefully wiped the steam off the mirror. He was half expecting Jingling Jim to pop up behind him and try to scare him. That didn't happen though, it was just Richard's reflection in the mirror. He took a deep breath and turned towards the hamper on the far wall to throw his towel in. That's when the steam took on the shape of Jingling Jim and the ghastly figure lunged at Richard. Richard went to jump back and slipped on some water, he ended up falling backwards and hit his head on the corner of the door frame, knocking him out.

Jingling Jim, knew this was his chance. While still in vapor form, he spiraled himself up and into the nose of Richard. Richard drew him in with each breath, and Jingling Jim started laughing, it was the laughing that woke Richard up.

"I think it's time you see a psychiatrist man," Richard told himself as he got up off the floor, then felt the back of his head and felt a knot. All the steam was gone out of bathroom, so Richard just grabbed his clothes and tossed them in the hamper, then left.

Richard decided to go for a walk instead of a bike ride, with his head hurting like it was, he wanted to take it easy. He made sure his momma was still asleep and then left.  Heat lightning filled the sky and there was so much cloud cover, Richard couldn't tell if there was a moon or not.  He couldn't wait for the coolness of October to arrive.  He hadn't walked extremely far and his shirt was already getting soaked with sweat.

He walked about mile into town and went right for the cemetery.  He felt like he had to be there, like something was drawing there or he was just curious for some reason.  He approached the cemetery and admired the black, iron fence with pointed post that surrounded it.  He walked up the arched gate that was anchored to brick pillars on each side of the gate.  There was a black sign with bronze lettering that gave the open and closing times and Richard was well past closing time, but the gate was open, so he went in.

A light sprinkle started falling as Richard slightly jogged on a walking path. The path went all around and through the cemetery. He had never been there before, and he didn't know why he didn't, but he felt comfortable being there.  He made a left turn that led down a center path and followed it to the end, near a fence line.  He then turned right and stopped to tie his shoe.  When he looked over to his left, he was staring at a gravestone with the name Linda McCurdy on it.

The gravestone looked more like a queen chest piece than gravestone.  It had chunks missing from it and moss filled the engraved letters of the name.  Richard felt drawn to it and cleaned off some of the overgrowth. He picked the moss from the letters and felt overwhelmed with sadness. He figured Linda McCurdy was related to Jim McCurdy but the gravestone simply had her name and 1993 on it, nothing indicating if she was a wife, mother, daughter or all three.

Richard finished cleaning off the gravestone and went back to jogging around the cemetery.  He then jogged out to The Gardens in time to see the nightshift security woman putting trash in the compactor.  He watched as she ran the compactor, then went back inside, only to return a few minutes later with a new load of trash.

She had on extra, tight khakis and danced around a little bit, not knowing Richard was watching. She danced to her little heart's desire, then when the compactor stopped, she stopped and headed in. Richard then jogged around town, finally heading back home and took another shower.

Richard awoke at the sound of his alarm. He didn't bother to shower because he took two the night before. He looked in the mirror, he had dark circles around his eyes, but he smiled anyways. His smile revealed some spots on his teeth. He looked confused and brushed his teeth, but the stains were still there, "Whatever!" he said as he rinsed his toothbrush off and put it up.

He got on his bike and pedaled a little slower to the gas station, he grabbed a few beef sticks and a few energy drinks. He was craving his special coffee again.

The air wasn't as thick with moisture so Richard wasn't soaked when he got to work. Ron was sitting down on the couch and Richard came to the door. Ron ran up and unlocked it, but didn't have smile on his face.

"Rough night?" Richard asked.

"Yeah, feels like it's a full moon around here," Ron said.

"Well," Richard looked up at the moon, "It's not yet, it's only going to get crazier from here then."

"Lord I hope not," Ron said as Richard walked to the elevator.

They rode down in silence and when the elevator opened, Richard could hear loud talking, almost yelling coming from down the hall. Richard paid no attention to it and went into his office. He clocked in and started a half pot of coffee with half energy drink. He noticed there were no notes for him this time, which he appreciated. He sat down and watched the cameras to see if he could see where the yelling was coming from. There was nothing in the halls nor behind the nurse's station. Whatever the raucous was, dispersed by the time Richard looked into it.

Then came the nightly knock and Richard walked Ron out and locked the door. He headed back down to shut the curtains and Leola was waiting for him by the elevator. She was wearing all black scrubs, a dark purple lipstick and smokey purple eye shadow. She was hesitant to talk to Richard but then she spoke up.

"I just wanted to apologize for what I said the other night, I didn't mean any disrespect," she said, with sadness in her eyes.

"It's okay princess, not everyone was brought up like me." Richard said and walked up the ramp trying not to pay attention to Leola.

"Please don't be that way, I seriously didn't mean anything bad by it. It just caught me off guard. My parents didn't want me around enough to have me living them any longer than normal. As soon as I turned eighteen, they kicked me out."

"Well, that's unfortunate. I am sorry that happened," Richard said and walked up to the window and pushed the button to close the curtains.

"Can we just act like that didn't happen? Please!" she pouted.

"I guess, I don't see why you're so worried about it," Richard said with some hate in his voice.

"I just think you're a nice person and I should have acted better."

"That you did, but it's over with, come to my office later after I make my rounds, I made some of my special coffee," Richard smiled.

"Oh lord! I don't see how you drink that, but I do kind of like it," She smiled, " I have to do a check," she said and walked away.

Richard walked out of the dining room, then walked down and around the inside of the garden. The flowers there smelled extra good that night. The pond there sounded more relaxing than normal. He finished his inside round and went and checked the lobby doors and the side door.

He went back down in his office for a cup of coffee and Leola came knocking a few seconds later with her coffee cup. Richard poured her a cup and took a sip of his, the bitter flavor filled his mouth and he liked it. Leola made a face from the taste, they chatted a little longer before Loela left.

Richard headed back to the dining room. He didn't notice it before but the floors were gross. There were stains all over, smeared in ketchup, grape jelly and a few other stains that looked almost like feces. Richard suspected the floor hadn't been swept or cleaned all day. Richard grew angry at the thought that it was just left for him. He moved the tables and chairs, then went to the cleaning room.

He added a little extra cleaning chemical because of all the stains and added a more abrasive scrubbing pad to the scrubber. He headed back to the dining room and moved slower than normal, he let the scrubbing pads do the work and he didn't suck up the soapy mixture at first, he let it sit as he made a few laps around. He then went and changed out the pads to a less aggressive pad and started sucking up the soapy water. He moved slow again, letting the pads act like buffing pads to bring a shine to the floor. He was happy with his work and apparently so did Leola.

"Wow, that looks good!" she said.

"Yeah, it was a mess, it was like they just left it for me to clean," Richard said upset.

"I don't know if they did it on purpose, maybe they got busy," Leola said.

"I don't think they got busy, I think they're just lazy," Richard said.

Leola stood there a second, then walked away. Richard went and got the tables and chairs and put them all back. He then cleaned out the scrubber and refilled it, then headed up to the lobby. It wasn't as bad as the dining room, but it was still bad. There were random pieces of Kleenex, it was almost like someone had wiped their nose and randomly dropped them.

Richard went back down and grabbed a broom and dustpan then went and swept the lobby, dumping the snot rags in the trash behind the receptionist desk. He went and then scrubbed the lobby. He repeated the process that he did with the lobby and gave it a deep scrub. He was thinking about the amount of disrespect, then was he was making a lap, he heard it, he heard Jingling Jim's voice.

"That's what it is Richard, blatant disrespect. They probably said leave it to the loser nightshift guy, the jannnnitorrrr, the wannabe cop, the loooooooser who still lives with his mom. I know that's what they say, I hear them. It's the same thing they said about me," Jingling Jim said.

"I believe it, I just want some respect," Richard said, he didn't want to be talking to Jingling Jim. He felt defeated though, he was tired and worn out from fighting. What didn't know what Jingling Jim was feeding him those emotions, like spoon feeding a baby.

"You're not going to get it, you're going to have to take it, just like you did before when we were a team. You saw the look of respect right before they passed, didn't you?"

"You're right, I did," Richard agreed, somewhat in a trance, still walking with the scrubber.

"Did you feel the respect they gave you, the rush, the power?"

"I did." Richard mumbled.

"Don't you want more of it?"

"I do," Richard said and was in a such a trance that he ran into the receptionist desk, "Shit!" he said to himself as he stopped the scrubber. He looked and there wasn't any damage to the receptionist desk, but the track that held the squeegee was bent, "God dammit Richard! Watch what you're doing."

Luckily, Richard didn't have much more to go before he finished it. He was able to complete the lobby with minimal streaks, then went and cleaned the machine. He left a note for Mark that he messed up the scrubber. It was on his way back to his office that Leola stopped him.

"Hey, Mr. Miller is having an issue with his bed, said it's been squeaking and keeping him awake. I was wondering if you could look at it, so he leaves us alone."

"Yeah, I'll look at it," Richard said.

He went back to the janitors closet and grabbed a screwdriver and adjustable wrench on the shelf and headed back out to Leola, "What's his room number?"

"E-Zero" she said.

E-Zero was right next to a little lobby that led to the hallway, that led to the kitchen. He went down and knocked on the door, "Hello Mr. Miller, I'm here to take a look at your bed."

"Well it's about damned time, what am I supposed to do, stay up all night?" Mr. Miller yelled and whipped the door open, "Well come in!" Mr. Miller was a little taller than Richard. He wore a black toupee on the top of his head, but didn't bother dying his sides of his hair black, and left them grey. He had a thick, black mustache, that stuck about inch over each side of his mouth. He had on blue and white striped pajamas and white slippers.

Richard followed Mr. Miller into his bedroom, "See," Mr. Miller pushed the bed and it squeaked.

"Ah, it seems it's just loose, luckily I bought the right tools for the job," Richard smiled.

"It doesn't matter what you brought, if you're not smart enough to use them," Mr. Miller said hatefully.

"Okay!" Richard said and knelt, he put the Phillips-head screwdriver on the screwhead and the adjustable wrench on the nut and started turning. He got the right side tightened up and was working on the left side when Mr. Miller walked up too close and hovered over him.

"You sure you know what you're doing?" Mr. Miller asked. Then Richard heard Mr. Miller make a slurping noise and felt something warm and wet on the back of his neck.

"What the hell?" Richard asked and shot up, almost bumping into Mr. Miller.

"YOU ALMOST KNOCKED ME OVER!" Mr. Miller yelled.

Richard wiped the back of his neck and put his hand out, "YOU DROOLED ON THE BACK OF MY NECK!" Richard yelled back.

"Well, I can't help it I drool," Mr. Miller grumbled and wiped his mouth, his face red with anger.

"You wouldn't have drooled on me if you weren't standing over me," Richard grumbled back.

"This is my room, I'll stand over whomever I please," Mr. Miller puffed his chest up.

"Then fix your own damn bed!" Richard said and tried walking by Mr. Miller.

"Nobody talks to me like that," Mr. Miller said and grabbed onto Richard's shoulder and spun him around. He wasn't expecting Richard to plunge the screwdriver, handle deep, into his head, but that's exactly what Richard done.

There was a sickening, crack, and a pop as the shaft the of screwdriver sunk into Mr. Miller's skull. Mr. Miller's eyes rolled into the back of his head and he started to fall over, Richard caught him and eased him onto his bed. Richard grabbed Mr. Miller's feet and put them on the bed as well. Richard pulled the screwdriver out and watched as blood trickled down the side of Mr. Miller's head and onto the white pillow.

"Damn, guess I'm gonna have to throw that out as well," Richard said to himself.

He walked out of Mr. Miller's room and walked down to the janitor's closet, keeping the screwdriver out of sight and washed the blood off of it and put it back on the shelf next to the adjustable wrench. He then washed his hands and scrubbed underneath his nails and looked at the trash cart, then the time, "Close enough!" he said even thought it was fifteen minutes early.

He grabbed the cart and got the trash from the west side of hall, it was a lot, but he smashed it down, then got the east hall trash and smashed it down again. He started heading towards the kitchen. He stopped at E-Zero and looked around, then quickly pushed the cart into Mr. Miller's room. He took out some trash, picked Mr. Miller up and his pillow and tossed them in the cart, then tossed the loose trash on top of Mr. Miller. Richard opened the door and looked down the hall, Leola just went into the bathroom, so Richard made his move. He backed out into the hallway, pulling out the cart, blocking the view of the trash cart from anyone down the hall.

He walked briskly down the hall and into the kitchen. There he stopped and looked around, "What the hell do I do now?"

"Why don't you look and see what's for lunch tomorrow?" he heard Jingling Jim say.

Richard looked around and found a large, dry erase board that had the weeks menu on it. They were going to have hamburgers for lunch the next day. Richard smiled as he then went and investigated one of the coolers and found four, five-gallon trays of hamburger. He took half the hamburger out of each tray and tossed it in his cart. He looked around again and found an industrial meat grinder. He didn't know anything about butchering or grinding but Jingling Jim did and took the wheel away from Richard.

"Let me show you how it's done son," Richard said to himself. He went and grabbed a filet knife and got to work. He sliced and diced chunks of Mr. Miller off. The trash was compacted enough that it stopped the blood from leaking through the bottom of the cart. He took and mixed parts of Mr. Miller with the hamburger in the grinder.  The hum of the machine and the squishing sound of Mr. Miller was relaxing to Richard.

He mixed the hamburger and Mr. Miller together and put all the meat back in the trays, replaced the saran wrap on them and put the trays back. He then washed his hands and made sure he didn't have any blood splatter on him, keeping the body in the trashcan helped with the blood not getting everywhere.  There wasn't much left of Mr. Miller, his face, skeleton, and entrails, which Richard made sure not to cut into. He then went and dumped the kitchen trash on the dock, over the remains of Mr. Miller.  He then took the cart and headed to the compactor.

It was so easy to get rid of Mr. Miller, Richard was surprised. As he dumped Mr. Miller's remains into the compactor, Jim let go of control and let Richard take back over somewhat.  He held onto the part of Richard that felt remorse and buried it deep.  He didn't want Richard feeling remorse, he needed Richard to stay tough and not show weakness with feelings, but he needed him physically weak so he could maintain his body.

There came the audible crunch of Mr. Miller's skeleton being crushed from the force of the hydraulics and Richard snapped out of his daze.  He smiled when he heard the crunching again and looked at the inside of his cart, blood streaked the sides and inside front of the cart, "Gonna have to give you a bath ol' lady," he said and started pushing the cart back in.  He took it straight to the janitor's closet, tipped it up and sprayed it out carefully as to not splatter blood all over him and the walls.  He then sprayed the inside of the cart with bleach, once again carefully, so he didn't get any on him.  He put the hose down the drain and left it for fifteen minutes or more, with hot water, to make sure all the blood washed away.  He looked at the time after he was done and realized it was almost time for the second trash run.

He walked out and checked the west hall and it wasn't bad enough to do another trash run.  So, he skipped it and headed to his office.  He reheated the cold coffee in the microwave and took a seat.  He reviewed the cameras and watched as, instead of him going into Mr. Millers room, that he simply just walked on by with the trash cart.  He laughed loudly, a little too loudly and maniacally.  There came a knock on his door.  He pushed himself over in his chair instead of getting up and opened the door.

Leola stood there with her coffee cup, "What are you laughing about?"

"Just saw a funny video is all," he said, "Wanting seconds, are we?"

"It's gross but it peps me up," she smiled, Richard smiled back and that's when Leola noticed his teeth, they were discolored, and they never were before, but she didn't say anything.

"I was wondering if one day after work, you'd like to go get a coffee or something?" Leola asked.

"One of these days, I say next Monday morning?"

"That sounds great!" Leola said, took a sip of her coffee, she smiled, left Richard's office and headed back up towards the nurse station.

Richard went back to looking at videos until it was time to let Brad in.  Brad was his normal, flamboyant, self.  He smiled at Richard and when Richard smiled back, he also noticed the discoloration in Richard's teeth.  Richard walked Brad down with no conversation and went to his office to wait for Mark.

Mr. Latrell was sound asleep, when suddenly he was jarred awake.  A sense of panic came over him, images of Jingling Jim flashed before him.  He screamed out and grabbed his chest, then fell out of his bed.  He was too terrified to move, his hands cramped up.  The evil was back with Richard and he knew it.  He screamed out again and this time Michelle came running in.

"Mr. Latrell, what are you doing?" she asked.

"THE EVIL IS BACK! THE EVIL IS BACK!" Mr. Latrell yelled, his face distorted in fear.

"MR. LATRELL, YOU NEED TO CALM DOWN!" Michelle said, but Mr. Latrell was in a fit and she needed help to try to get him up off the floor.  She ran and got her wonder drug, ran back to Mr. Latrell's room and gave him the shot.  Once Mr. Latrell calmed down, she grabbed a bed sheet, turned Mr. Latrell on his side, tucked the bed sheet under him, and rolled him towards her, then pulled the bed sheet out on the other side.

Michelle got up and tracked down Leola, she was going ask Richard but didn't.

Richard was in the middle of cleaning up his office when the knock came to his door. He opened the door and there stood Mark, looking worse for wear.  He didn't have his hat on and his thin, white hair was disheveled.  He had dark circles under his eyes so dark, Richard wondered if they were black eyes.

"Rough night?" Richard asked.

"I guess you can say that. Anything happen last night I need to know about?" Marks voice was raspy.

"No, but I saw they're having hamburgers today for lunch on the menu in the kitchen.  I wish they'd have good food like that for me on nightshift," Richard said and smiled.

"Damn son, brush your teeth, have you been eating ass all night?" Mark said, not holding back.

"Nah, chocolate chip cookies," Richard said and stopped smiling.

"Smells like ass!" Mark said and walked away.

Richard went and clocked out, took a swig of water, swished it around in his mouth and spit it out in a half-assed attempt to rinse his mouth.  He then went and got on his bike and went for a ride.

The morning was cooler than normal, which felt good to Richard.  He found himself going towards the cemetery.  He made a couple laps around the cemetery, passing Linda's gravestone a few times.  He then went and rode to a burger joint just outside of Yertzville.  After making some hamburgers he was craving them.  They served burgers 24/7 and he ordered a double burger with cheese, and bacon and chili-cheese fries, with a large soda to drink.

He sat on the yellow curb that was right next to highway 31.  He sat cross-legged, keeping his feet off the highway and started wolfing down his burger.  He had one bite left and looked up as a red, SUV started heading towards him.  Just as it was about to pass, he threw the last bite at the SUV's side and it stuck.  He then started on his fries, noisily licking the cheese from his fingers.  He chugged his soda, then left his mess in the grass by the road.  He rode home afterwards, ignored the dishes in the sink and went to his room.

He started to dream and it was strange to him. He was sitting in a chair, tied up, in a room with a light above his head. Jingling Jim appeared at the edge of the lights circle, walking in just enough to highlight his face.  Then Jingling Jim started laughing as Richard realized it was over for him, he sobbed and put his head down. Tears of defeat fell upon the floor and when Richard woke up, he wasn't Richard.

# Chapter Twenty: Tuesday, Mrs. Jaque

## and the Pond

Richard woke up when he heard his momma yelling at him for not doing dishes, he just smiled as she ranted from the kitchen. He stayed awake after that and watched as his alarm went off.  He got up, didn't bother messing with his hair, he brushed his teeth, but spit out blood.  He put on his grey pants and shirt that he wore the night before and got on his bike.

He went to the gas station, picked up a case of energy drinks and balanced them on his bike as he rode.  It was a tricky ride, and he thought he was going to drop them at one point. He was covered in sweat by the time he got work, and was more than happy when Ron opened the door.

Ron was wearing regular street clothes instead of a uniform, which caught Richard off guard but ultimately ignored it, "Drinking heavy tonight?" Ron joked about the case of energy drinks.

"Should last me through the night," Richard joked back, "Anything happen tonight?"

"Nope, well Mrs. Jaque wants to be let into the garden at five-thirty so she can watch the sunrise in there.  You did miss a really good supper, they had leftover hamburgers from lunch, they were awesome. Oh! Mr. Miller disappeared from the building so I believe the state might be showing up this week. Too many deaths and disappearances in a short amount of time."

"I doubt they come on third shift," Richard said, scared he may have been caught.

"I've worked in medical facilities before, they rarely stay over on second shift, and never nightshift, so you're safe.  Just odd how Mr. Miller walked out of here without anyone seeing him, the only reason they knew he left was because of the cameras showed him leaving. He went right up the elevators, right after you left and walked right out the front doors."

"Thank god for those then," Richard said with a little sarcasm in his voice.

They got off the elevator and Richard put his energy drinks in the fridge in his office.  He took one out, and poured straight energy drink into the coffee maker, no water whatsoever.  He made a pot of the mixture and when he tried it, his face puckered, "I like it," he said and smiled.

He then walked over to his thermostat and turned it down to sixty-degrees.  He propped his feet up for a few minutes, while he went through the camera footage.  He found the footage Mr. Miller walking out.  It was strange to see and the footage skipped a lot when Mr. Miller walked.  Mr. Miller swung his arms twitchingly as he walked and at one point, right before he walked out the front door, Mr. Miller stopped and looked at the camera.

"What are you looking at you dead piece of shit!" Richard sneered and then came Ron's knock of three thumps, a pause and then a fourth thump. Richard got up and opened the door.

"Ready when you are boss!" Ron said.

"Let the shit-show begin," Richard smirked and he walked Ron up to the front, locked the doors and headed back down to shut the curtains.

On his way, he noticed the floor was losing its sheen, a little. He pressed the button to close the curtains and started putting up the tables and chairs.  He had everything up and started walking out when Michelle stopped him.

"You okay?" she asked with a concerned look on her face.

"Yeah, why?"

"You look a little pale."

"Just haven't been sleeping well is all," Richard replied and smiled.

Michelle looked repulsed and crinkled her nose, "You ain't been brushing those nasty-ass teeth as well, damn son, your breath stinks! I'm going to get you a mint," Michelle said and walked away.

Richard was slightly offended, then breathed into hand and smelled it, "Eh, I've smelled worse." He shrugged his shoulders and walked to the garden. He made a lap around and walked across the catwalk to admire the fish and the pond. He then locked it up, with Ron's words still in his head about Mrs. Jaque wanting the garden open at five-thirty so she could see the sun rise.

He then went and got his wax ready and went about putting a thin layer of wax on the dining room floor. He moved swiftly and focused, there were no antics from the residents yet, but the night was still young. He finished up the dining room and checked out the lobby, it wasn't nearly as bad so he decided he would just scrub it. He headed back down to the janitor's closet and stopped off at his office for a second. On his desk was a pack of mint chewing gum. He took two pieces out and put them in his mouth and tucked the rest of the pack into his shirt pocket.

He put the blue, cleaning chemical in the scrubber and added the water, when he heard Jingling Jim, "Whatchya gonna do tonight?"

"I might take it easy, I'm not having any problems, so why cause any?" Richard said.

"Because chaos is fun! What about that bitch Mrs. Jaque? She's wanting in the garden at five-thirty, you don't open up the garden that early? Why let Mrs. Jaque boss you around?"

"I'm not letting her boss me around, I'm just fulfilling a request," Richard said and yawned.

"Well, fine, but if you let her in there, tell her to go to the rose garden, I'm sure they look pretty this time of year."

"Oh, okay, I will," Richard said and thought it was odd that Jingling Jim was giving up so easily.  Richard finished filling the scrubber and took it up to the lobby first to let the wax fully dry.

He scrubbed the lobby, looking out into the parking lot as he done so. He was happy that he wasn't going to be bothered by Jingling Jim, and part of him got to thinking about the rose garden and why Jingling Jim, wanted Mrs. Jaque to go see it, "Well, maybe he was just being nice," Richard said as he made the final lap around the lobby.

He cleaned out the scrubber, then took the propane buffer up to the dining room and started buffing the floor.  He went side to side with the buffer and let it glide smoothly across the floor. He was doing such a good job, that even Jingling Jim let him alone to work. He was able to get half the chairs and tables back out before it was time to do a garbage run.

He grabbed the trash cart and before he started, he took his keys out of his pocket and let them dangle he was rather enjoying the sound they made when he walked.  He checked the west hall closet and it was packed, it looked as if second shift didn't do a trash run and forgot to tell him.  Richard loaded in the trash and it was about level with the brim of the cart.  He realized then he was going to make several trash runs that night.   He headed outside and the minute he opened the door it started to rain.

"Great!" Richard said as he rushed to the compactor, as the rain beat down on him, soaking him.  He threw the trash in and didn't wait for it to compact, before rushing back inside.  He stood at the door and listened for the compactor to stop before shutting the door.

"BOO!" he heard someone say as he felt hands on his hips from behind him, causing him to jump.

He turned around and there stood Leola, "Did I scare ya?" she asked and smiled.

"Ya, you got me good," Richard said, but didn't smile.

"Man, it's really raining out isn't it?"

"Yeah, and trash rooms are full so I'll be getting wet as hell going in and out."

"Yeah, there was a party on second shift for one of the residents and I guess Ron got sidetracked from what I was told."

"Well, Ron didn't mention shit about it to me, would have been nice," Richard said a little angry.

"That wasn't very nice of him, a heads-up would have been nice," Leola said smiled, but once again, Richard didn't smile. He just quietly chewed on the gum Michelle gave him.

"I'm going to go get east hall now, I hope it's not as bad as west hall," Richard said and pushed the cart towards the elevator.

"Can I ride down with you?" Leola asked, "I really don't want to take the stairs."

"I don't see why not, there will be room."

They both boarded the elevator and rode down in silence. Leola didn't say anything but Richard could see her crinkling her nose from time to time as if she was smelling something rotten. Richard took in a deep, yet hidden breath and couldn't smell anything out of the normal. He shrugged it off in his head, and waited for the elevator to open, in which Leola hurried off. It could have been the trash cart stinking for all Richard knew. He pushed the cart out and went down east hall and it was just as full as west hall. So, he loaded it up, once again to the brim of the cart.

It was another rainy trip to the compactor and he repeated his steps from before. He loaded in the trash, quickly, pressed the button to activate it, then ran back to the door and waited for it to finish. He was enjoying the rain, he just wasn't enjoying being in it. Leola didn't scare him this time, so he hung out a few extra minutes listening to the rain hit off the metal compactor. He was really starting to crave a cigarette. He decided if it wasn't raining when he got off work he was going to buy some.  He finally decided to head back in and get the trash from the kitchen.

As Richard was walking down east hall, Michelle mentioned something about his keys being noisy, but Richard blocked it out and continued his way.  He stopped when he got to dock, it was a mess, there were three more trashcans than normal and the grease can, all completely full.

Richard started with the grease can, the smell radiating from it was horrible.  It was so full that when he tried to move it, it spilled on the floor.  He tried to avoid it but ended up slipping on it anyway and landed hard on his back.  The wind was knocked out of him and Richard struggled to breathe.  He was finally able to get up after a few minutes, his left arm, sleeve and shoulder were covered in grease.

"You have key to Tim's office, do something," he heard Jingling Jim say.

"Like what?" Richard responded.

"I don't know, let's look in his office, I'm sure we can figure something out," he said.

Richard went through his keys and found the one that opened Tim's office.  He went in and looked around and didn't see much he could until he spotted the coffee pot.

"How about you piss in the coffee pot, he won't know the difference in color."

"Yeah, it does look like a gravity feed coffee pot, so he will have to add a pot to get a pot, pushing the urine water through." Richard said and smiled.

"Attaboy!"

Richard carefully unplugged the coffee machine, and put it down on the floor.  He opened the top, then took aim.  He started to urinate through the grate and heard some water being pushed through into the pot as he done so.  When he was done, he put the coffee machine back where he got it, plugged it in, then dumped what little urine water was in the pot and walked out of Tim's office.

He went back and managed to dump the grease can and cleaned it out.  Then he took his utility knife and cut halfway through on the back side.  Next time it got full, he was hoping it would burst and the mess would be the kitchen staffs to clean up.  He turned his attention to the trashcans and noticed half-eaten hamburgers on top.  He smiled as he pulled the first bag out of the trash.  It was heavy and he had to lift a little extra to get the bag out.  He didn't even set it down to tie it off, just carried it over into the cart.  He had to repeat the process for the rest of the trashcans.  The cart was once again full, but fuller than before and a little hard to push. Then on the way up, a wheel started squeak.

"Man, you're just noisy tonight aren't you.  You have your keys jingling and wheels squeaking, don't you know people are trying to sleep?" Michelle asked with a little bit of anger in her voice.

"I don't know what your problem is, but you can get off my ass tonight," Richard said.  Michelle looked offended and for once, didn't say anything in return, just stared at Richard like she couldn't believe he just said what he said.

Richard went on his way and took the last load of trash up.  It was still raining, but not as hard, which was good because it took him a little extra to lift the heavy trash bags into the compactor.  After about twenty minutes, counting having to take a break from the heavy lifting, he was able to compact the trash and head inside and wait by the door, then listened for it to finish compacting.  He was drenched and didn't want to sit in his office like that so, he waited about half an hour to dry off a little bit, then he headed to office and warmed up his mixture.

Richard reviewed some footage, but he mostly watched Leola on camera.  He watched as she checked only three rooms on each hall and brought out trash from them to place in the closets.  He zoomed in on her face, then her chest, then her backside and smiled creepily as he watched.  He stayed in his office until it was time for the second trash run.

He walked down to the janitor's closet and sprayed the wheel on the cart with oil, before heading out so Michelle didn't gripe about it squeaking but he was going to be damned if he was going to put his keys away.  There were enough trash bags that Richard felt he needed to continue the second trash run.  The east hall was slightly fuller than the west hall, which seemed to be the norm.

The rain was just a mist by the time Richard got back out to the compactor. He was tossing the trash in when he noticed a shed on the property.  Heat lightning flashed in the sky, Richard thought he saw an axe sitting outside the door, which was weird because he didn't notice it earlier, then again there wasn't any lightning earlier, so he wouldn't have been able to see it.  He focused again and when the heat lightning happened again the axe was gone.  Richard stepped away from the compactor and walked towards the shed. He brought out his flashlight and shone it on the shed.  There was no axe and the lock was still on the door.

Richard turned around and walked back to the compactor. He grabbed his cart and headed in, making sure to wipe his feet before he headed in so he didn't track mud into the lobby.  He put the cart away and went back to his office, he reheated the last of his mixture and sat down.  He looked at his watch and had about an hour before he had to open the garden for Mrs. Jaque.  He propped his feet up again and watched the cameras until it was time.

He left his office at five-twenty and started walking down west hallway towards the garden doors when he saw and old lady, she had all white, short, curly hair.  She was wearing a pink bath robe with matching slippers.  He could see the smile on her face from all the way down the hallway.

"Ohh you must be Richard?" Mrs. Jaque asked and extended her feeble, veiny little hand for Richard to take.

"That I am, I'm going to unlock the garden for you," Richard smiled and for once someone didn't flinch at the sight.

"Oh, gracious, I'm so excited. I always watch it from my room, but I've always wanted to watch the sunrise from on top of the catwalk and let the sun kiss my naked body," Mrs. Jaque smiled.

Richard stopped unlocking the door and looked at her, "What?"

"As soon as the sun comes up, I'm dropping this robe, now don't go opening those curtains, I don't want you peeking," she giggled.

"I...uh...I won't," Richard said and shook his head a little to rid the thought from his head, "But, you should definitely check out the roses before you leave.  Heard it from good source, they're really pretty when the sun hits them."

"Thanks for recommendation honey, I sure will check them out," Mrs. Jaque smiled and patted Richard's arm as he finished unlocking the doors for her.

Mrs. Jaque walked in and Richard shut the doors behind her, "It'll probably be the last thing you do, you old hag," Richard mumbled to himself as he walked away.

Mrs. Jaque walked up on the catwalk, directly over the pond. She looked up and waited for the sun to rise.  When the sun started creeping down into the garden. Mrs. Jaque dropped her pink robe, exposing her age-ridden body.  She outstretched her arms and shut her eyes as the sun crept up the catwalk, then up her body, shining through her eyelids and thin, flappy skin on her arms.  She smiled and giggled, then picked up her robe and put it back on.  She looked down at the roses and they were sparkling in the sunlight.

"Those sure are pretty, I think I will pick me one," she said and shuffled down the steps, walked up to the rose garden and carefully plucked a rose from the bush.  She turned her back and smelled the rose.

She was enjoying the rose smell when two thorned tentacles shot out of the rose bush, two wrapped around Mrs. Jaque's midsection and one wrapped around her throat and squeezed it tight before she could scream.  The tentacles pulled in opposite directions of each other, and Mrs. Jaque's head began to separate from her body.  The thorns acted like saws and cut through her flesh, but stopped before cutting through the spinal cord.  The tentacles pulled and Mrs. Jaque's spine separated from her hips and was pulled out of her body. Her spine with her head on it, closely resemble a rose that had been plucked from a bush.

The tentacles pulled the body, head and spine into the ground.  Then, a massive, composted soil, tongue formed and lapped up all the spilled blood.  There was no trace left of Mrs. Jaque, not even her cute, fluffy, pink slippers.  All the roses returned to their original positions and anyone walking in there wouldn't be able to tell that Mrs. Jaque ever set foot in there.

Richard was cleaning up his office when there came a knock on the door, he had let Brad in already, and figured it would have been Mark, but it was Leola instead.

"Have you seen Mrs. Jaque?" she asked.

"Nope, let her in the garden and left," Richard said.

"Hmmm, maybe she's in the public restroom," Leola said.

"Maybe," Richard said and cleaned out his coffee pot, "Who knows with this place, they seem to be leaving and dying every time I turn around."

"Yeah, this place is going down quick, heard a rumor about State coming in."

"I heard the same rumor, but I'm not worried about it, they don't come on nightshift."

"True, I think I'm more worried for this place, it just got opened up, and could be shut down rather quickly."

"Eh, security and nursing jobs are everywhere, I wouldn't worry too much!" Richard said and dried the inside of coffee cup out with piece of paper towel.

"I guess you're right, I just really like my job."

"It'll be the same job, just somewhere else."

Leola realized she wouldn't be able to relay the meaning of her message to Richard, he was coming across as extremely negative. She got quiet and slowly shut Richard's door.  She walked back up the ramp and went to the public bathroom and knocked on doors. No one answered, but as she started to head down the hall to Mrs. Jaque's room, the dayshift CNA stopped and started asking her questions about her night and after that it was time to clock out.

She got in her car and sat there for a minute, she couldn't shake the thought that Mrs. Jague, like Mr. Miller had up and disappeared in the in the same week. To her they always seemed to disappear right before it was time to leave.  She started her car and slowly drove off, passing Richard as she drove down the road.

She didn't wave at him, she could tell something was off. Then again, had acted weird the whole time she had worked there and started to wonder if something was mentally off with him.  She was beginning to get worried, but decided to clear her head before driving to her trailer.

Leola grew up poor, she worked hard for everything she had, so her little trailer, that she paid for in cash, was her pride and joy. She was housed on a dead-end street in the trailer court.  It wasn't very big, but being painted a dark green with grey shutters, made it bigger than anything in the world to her.  She always relax in her jacuzzi tub when she got home and that day was no different.  She stripped down, got in and let the bubbles massage her worries away.

# Chapter Twenty-one: Wednesday and

## Tim's Oopsie Daisey

Richard went straight home sat on his bed all day in vegetative state. Maria checked on him, but stayed by the door and peeked in.  She prayed continuously every time she checked on him and even when she didn't check on him, she prayed.  She turned her recliner around to face Richards room and read her bible up until noon when she dozed off.

Richard stared at his T.V. that wasn't turned on.  His breathing went shallow for a while, his eyes glazed over and a small growl came from his mouth as he breathed.  He watched as the sun got bright, then started to dim.  He stayed in the vegetative state until his alarm went off.  The glaze on his eyes disappeared and he looked over at his alarm and stared at it for a minute before shutting it off.  He decided to take a shower then, decided to scrub his teeth so no one complained about his breath.

He scrubbed and spit, blood and brown, blood and brown were all that came out, every time he spit.  He took the mouthwash and took a big swig, the burning was so bad that he immediately spit it out and groaned out in pain.  His mouth felt as if he had ingested the sun itself.

He layered on the deodorant and the cologne he realized what the smell was, he realized, it was rot.  His teeth were rotting, and he was rotting from the inside.

"It's not rot boy, it's the musk of a man!" Jingling Jim said.

"It smells like rot to me," Richard looked at his rotting teeth in the mirror.

"Nah, boy, its musk, trust me. I smelled like that for years and it drove the women nuts," Jingling Jim laughed.

"Yeah, but probably not in the way you think it did," Richard laughed. He was getting along with his parasitic ghost.

Richard walked into the kitchen, got into the fridge, chugged some milk out of the gallon jug and when he put it back, the milk was tainted red, then headed on his way out.  He rode down to the gas station, and grabbed three packs of cigarettes.

The weather wasn't rainy, but extremely moist.  Richard's shirt was sticking to him halfway through the trip.  He had to stop and wipe the sweat from his brow and pulled his wet shirt off from his chest.  He went back to riding his bike, after a few minutes of rest and made it to work, slightly later than normal.

Ron was waiting for him outside when he pulled, "Damn man, I thought you called in," Ron joked.

"Had to stop, this weather sucks.  I thought after the other morning it was going to start cooling off!"

Richard walked inside with Ron and felt the instant cool of air conditioning, "That feels good, you have anything to tell me?"

"It didn't come from me, but Mark told me Tim was on a rampage.  He said his grease can split in half and dumped all over ground, started blaming everyone except himself. I was hoping he would get fired, but we didn't get so lucky. Also the rumor turned out to be true, state showed up," Ron said as he pushed the button on the elevator.

"Well, he has plenty of other trashcans, he's proven that point. I ain't too worried about state, they can suck it for all I care" Richard rolled his eyes.

"Get this, he even went to James and Sheila over ordering better water filters because his coffee tasted bitter, what an idiot."

Richard just laughed and couldn't stop laughing as he got off the elevator.  He made his nightly mixture and sat down for a few minutes before the nightly knock came.  He walked Ron up and locked the doors.  He then headed back down to the dining room, shut the curtains then went and locked the garden doors.

He examined the hallways, there were a few stains here and there, that he was going to have extract.  The back end of east hall, where it turned into the hallway for the kitchen, was going to have to be completely extracted.  It was black, and when Richard reached down and touched it, it had a greasy feel to it.  Tim had tracked grease from the kitchen down east hall.

"That son-of-a-bitch!" Richard shook his head and stood up.

Richard went back to his office and got in his top drawer.  He took out two pieces of gum and put them in his mouth.  His mouth was overtaken with minty flavor which he didn't care for, but figured it would save him some grief later.  He headed down to the janitor's closet and grabbed a spray bottle with a cleaning agent in it and a buffer.

He left the janitor's closet with the spray bottle and bonnet/buffer and sprayed the grease spots with it and let them sit. He went down and soaked the back of east hallway with the cleaning solution.  He then went back with bonnet/buffer and worked the stains out of the carpet. After he was done with the smaller spots, he focused on the disaster on the back of east hall.  He grabbed a few more bonnet pads because he knew it wasn't going to come clean on the first try.

He bonneted the carpet until first trash run.  He had went through the extra pads he brought, but the stains were coming up. He done the trash on west and east hall but didn't get the trash in the kitchen because he didn't want to track the cart through the carpet.

The west hall trash wasn't too bad, but east hall filled it up and Richard noticed there was, what looked like scraps from the kitchen in the east hall garbage.  Richard feared what the kitchen looked like, but turned his focus back on the trash run.  Richard took the trash up and lit up a cigarette the minute he stepped outside the door.

The weather was worse than before, Richard was squirming because of how bad his clothes were sticking to him.  He loaded up the trash in the compactor, puffed away on his cigarette, letting the smoke fill his lungs, and blowing the smoke out his nose.  He flipped the cigarette at the normal spot as the trash compacted and smiled. He took the cart back down, sprayed it out and went back to the carpet.

The air conditioning felt good to Richard, but he was still working up a little sweat working the bonnet/buffer back and forth. He finally went and got the extractor to start extracting the chemical and dirt from the carpet.  The soft hum of the extractor was somewhat relaxing to Richard, but the suction noise was kind of annoying.  It took a total of three trips and up until second trash run for Richard to get the carpet looking like it was before.  He put the fans to it and done the second trash run.

As Richard suspected, the kitchen dock was trashed.  There was grease all over the dock floor and the trashcans looked as if they've been kicked over, spilling its contents halfway across the dock floor.  Richard got the trash that was in cans and didn't bother getting the ones that were knocked over.  He was leaving that for Tim and was going to make sure Tim knew about it.

"Why don't you stay in confront him, or scare him, I bet we could scare him to death," Jingling Jim said.

"How would we do that?" Richard asked.

"It's dark on the dock and he has to turn on the lights, I'm sure we could hide until then.  You can clock out, come around and come in through the dock doors since you have the keys. It'll be fun."

"Yeah, that sounds like a good idea!" Richard said and loaded up the last bit of trash, then took the cart out and up the kitchen dock, so he didn't track up the carpet.  He took and unloaded the trash in the compactor. The compactor rumbled like it usually had done, then a long, strenuous, whine came from the compactor. The whole machine shook, then stopped working.  A hose flew off from the side and sprayed hydraulic fluid all over the place, narrowly missing Richard.  Richard, dodged the flailing hose, hurried over and hit the emergency stop button. The hydraulic fluid quit spraying everywhere and the hose stopped moving then fell to the side of the machine. The metal, hydraulic connector made a loud thud as it hit the side.

"Well, isn't this just great!" Richard said stepping over the broken hose, "Guess, I'll have to let Mark know."

He walked through the grass back to the side door, just to make sure to get any fluid off his shoes that night have accidentally gotten on there.  He brought the cart down, sprayed it and put it up for the night.  He then went down and checked the carpet.  The fans were working, but not quick enough, it was going to be close to the end of the shift before the carpet was dry.

"Hey, gotta cup of coffee for sad, single girl?" Leola asked Richard as he walked by.

"Yeah, I need to make some more or I could just give you an energy drink," Richard laughed.

"I'll take it, shit why not?" Leola flipped her hair and made a silly face.

Richard nodded for her to follow him and they went into his office. He opened the fridge, grabbed two energy drinks, and handed one to Leola.  She looked at the green and red can, with 3D, black letters that spelled PURGE.

"These any good?" she asked.

"A little bitter but they help," Richard smiled and took a big swig of his.

Leola took a big swig of hers and crinkled up her face, "Lord, that's horrible," she proclaimed and then took another sip, "Thank you!"

"How's it been going tonight?" Richard took a sip of his drink.

"Mr. Latrell is on one, he's been horrible for a week or so, but now he just shouts, "THE EVIL IS BACK!" all the time, then speaks in Latin, who the hell does that?"

"Old, washed-up, Catholic priests," Richard answered.

"True there," Leola took another sip, "Well, I better get back to the paperwork, that shit sucks."

He decided to make a round and check the outside doors. After making sure they were locked, he went back to his office and waited until after he let Brad in, to pull the fans. After he pulled the fans, it was almost time for Mark to show up. He cleaned up the coffee pot quickly and washed his hands. Then came the knock he was waiting for and there stood Mark.

He had on a grey work shirt, black pants and a hat, the dark circles under his eyes were fading, "How'd it go last night?" he asked, the odor of a freshly smoked cigarette filled Richard's nose.

"The trash compactor blew a hose, sounded like it jammed up before it did though," Richard explained.

"That piece of shit, I knew that was coming," Mark said and looked disgruntled.

"Tim, that asshole, tracked grease all the way down east hall, took me all night to get cleaned. I'm going to get going though, I'm tired, you have a good day," Richard said as Mark mumbled something under his breath.

There was a heavy dew on the grass that stuck to Richards shoes as he moved quickly to the dock ramp and made his way down and through a side door, then hid by the trashcans and waited.

Tim was running a little late; he spent too much time in the mirror, combing and recombing his hair.  He re-tucked in his green, red and pink plaid shirt, into his brown, corduroy pants and over shone his, brown, penny-loafers.  His fashion to say the least, was horrible, but to him he looked glorious.

He hustled towards the elevator, swiped his badge and pressed the button a half a dozen times before it came to him.  He got on, ran his fingers through his short hair, and pressed the button on the inside another half a dozen times before it closed and took him down.  He rushed up the ramp and almost ran into Mark.

"Watch where you are going…..idiot!" Mark grumbled.

Tim just turned around and smiled before turning back around and was practically speed walking to the clock-in clock, just inside the kitchen doors and just beat the time before he was late. He fumbled with the keys to his office, but finally found the key and unlocked his door.  The first thing he grabbed was the coffee pot and went to a sink that was right before the doors to the dock. As he was rinsing out his coffee pot, looked through one of the door's windows and saw that the kicked over trashcans weren't picked up.

"That lazy son-of-a-bitch," Tim said and used his badge to open the doors with his coffee pot still in his hands, "I'm about over that guy."

Tim looked at the grease on the floor and the trash, then something moved next to the trashcan that made him jump a little, "Damn mice! I'll squish your damned heads in," he said and took another step towards the trashcans.  He looked around to see if he could see any mice but he didn't.  Then, someone or something jumped out from behind the trashcans. Tim only got a brief look of the rotted, skull-like face with no eyes before he stepped back into some grease and slipped.  His feet flew out from underneath him and the landed on his side.  The coffee pot shattered on the side of his face and stuck in the side of this throat, cutting his jugular vein in the process.

Blood pumped out of his neck with each beat of his heart.  He was looking at the thing that scared him and before he lost consciousness, he saw the face of the thing clear up and Richard's face appear.  The blood started to drift towards Richard's feet so Richard stepped back and watched as the blood mixed with some of the grease and traveled to the drain.

"Guess your life, just went down the drain!" Jingling Jim said in Richard's head and they both started laughing.

Richard walked out the dock and stayed up against the building to stay out of the camera's view and made it to his bicycle unseen.  He sat down on the seat, lit up a cigarette and headed home.

# Chapter Twenty-Two: Thursday and

# The Hostile Takeover

Maria had breakfast waiting for Richard when he got home. She had chorizo sausage, eggs, beans, tortillas, bacon, all spread out for Richard. She just finished setting the breakfast out when she saw Richard coming up the driveway. She raced to her room and shut the door and no sooner she had done that, the front door opened. She eased herself into her bed and brought the covers up and pretended to be asleep.

Richard sat down and shoveled the food in his mouth, letting most of it fall out as he chewed. He downed the milk and orange juice, wiped his mouth, then belched. He left the dishes on the table and headed to his room. He took off his shirt and pants and tossed his work clothes off to the side of his bed. He got up on his bed and lay there staring at the T.V..

He started to doze off, then suddenly he was out. He soon, entered a dream state. In his dream he was standing in the incinerator room, by himself at first. Then the handle on the incinerator started to jiggle, it then popped up and the door swung open. A black, ash covered, foot appeared, then another one, then two hands popped out and grabbed onto the outside of the door. Then, the rest of the body came out and there stood Jingling Jim.

"Hello Richard!" Jingling Jim said, his eyes were bright red, like he had red lights for eyes.

"I'm finally getting sleep," Richard said, "And I'm not tied up this time." Jingling Jim started to walk around Richard.

"Well, I think after this dream, you'll get plenty of sleep," Jingling Jim said and smiled, showing his rotted teeth.

"What, why?" Richard asked, and followed Jingling Jim around.

"Because this dream is about to become a nightmare," Jingling Jim smirked.

Suddenly, ash covered tendrils shot out of the incinerator and wrapped around Richard's waist, wrists and ankles, searing his flesh and started pulling him back, "HEYY! WAIT, I THOUGHT WE WERE A TEAM?"

"We were, but I don't think you can do what needs to be done, besides, I'm tired of living in there, I believe it's your turn now."

The tendrils pulled Richard back, "NOOOOOOOOOOO!" He screamed out and tried to fight it, but he had no power against the evil darkness he was getting pulled into. He was soon pulled into the incinerator and the door slammed shut. Jingling Jim walked over and put the handle over the latch.

"Don't worry about the cold darkness, it'll be always be warm in there," Jingling Jim said, then he reached over and fired up the incinerator. Richard's screams filled the air, then only the crackling sound of the flames in the incinerator was heard. Jingling Jim started to laugh and it echoed in the room.

Richard's eyes opened and they were a stone-cold grey. He smiled and drool fell from the corner of his left lip. He looked at the clock and it was almost time for Richard to get up. He rolled out of bed and headed towards the shower. He barely turned on the hot water and when he got in the shower, the water running down his body turned black as if it were washing off years of ash.

He got dressed, didn't bother brushing or putting on deodorant. He walked out to the bike and looked at it, then tossed it down, went back and got the car keys. He then got in his mom's car, lit up a cigarette and started the car. It felt good to drive, easier on his leg muscles.

He pulled into work and parked in the handicapped parking spot, flipped the cigarette out the window and got out. Ron was standing at the door with a dumbfounded look on his face, his mouth agape.  It wasn't the first time the car was taken to Richard's work but it was still surprising to see.

"You got a car?" Ron asked.

"Yeah, I work too hard to have to ride a bike to work," Richard said.

"It's been a crazy evening, I kind of figured it was because of the full moon," Ron pointed to the moon.

"All sorts of bad things happened tonight," Richard said and smirked.

"This black sludge started backing up in most the tubs and sinks. I had to call a company out here to run a sewer snake.  Then all the lights started to flicker and kept flickering then finally stopped. The residents have been hateful and disrespectful.  Its been like nothing I've ever experienced before here," Ron said and scratched his head, "I guess I should tell about Tim," Ron paused.

"What about that jerk?"

"They found him dead on the dock.  He slipped on some grease and fell on his coffee pot," Ron said his voice a little shaky.

"Hmm, guess he won't be a problem anymore," Richard smirked.

Ron's eyes got big, like he couldn't Richard just said what he said, "I guess not. Oh! The compactor got fixed, something was jammed in it."

"That's good," Richard said.

They walked to the elevator in silence and rode down in silence as well.  They went their separate ways. Richard went into his office and made plain coffee for a change, no sugar, no energy drink, nothing to keep him awake, he didn't need to stay awake. The only reason Richard was kept awake was to weaken him down for the takeover.

Richard checked the video footage to see if he was caught on the cameras earlier, he wasn't.  A crooked smile formed on his face, he sniffed the air, "Sure does feel good to be back, fulltime."

He left the office and went about shutting the curtains, he looked over at Michelle, who hadn't said much to him all week, "These curtains stay shut ya hear?" he said.

"We don't mess with your damn curtains, dummy!" Michelle snapped and narrowed her eyes at Richard.

Richard just nodded, smirked, and walked out of the dining room, jingling his keys as he walked, "Jingling Jim McCurdy, done the residents dirty," he said and started whistling.

"You better quiet down, I ain't listening to that crap all night," Michelle said to Richard and all he did was whistle louder.

"I don't know what's wrong with him, but here lately he's been getting on my nerves," Michelle said to Leola.

"I might try to talk to him later, see what's going on," she said.

"Be careful, he's been giving me the heebie-jeebies," Michelle said and slightly shook her head, "There's something about his eyes, they seem different."

"I'll ask to see if he got contacts," Leola looked at Michelle with a questionable look on her face.

"Girl just be careful, like I said, here!" Michelle said and went through her purse, she produced a zebra-striped, mace canister, "Take this, just in case."

"You think I'll need this with Richard?" Leola was shocked.

"You never know!"

Leola took the mace and put it in the side pocket on her scrubs, then went about her nightly duties.

Richard walked down the hall and locked the garden doors and, on his way, back to the dining room to move the furniture for scrubbing, he knocked on a few resident's doors, just to disturb them.  He heard a couple doors open then slam shut and a small chuckle came out of his mouth.

He walked into the dining room and moved the tables and chairs into the closet, then went and got his scrubber.  He went back to the dining room and put the pads down but not the squeegee.  He made a few laps letting the pads do a deep scrub, then on the final lap, dropped the squeegee.  He sucked up the water, then went to drain it, but instead of shutting the squeegee motoroff down the hallway, he kept it going.  Once again, a few more residents opened their doors to look and see where the noise was coming from.

He made sure when he went through the door that led to the janitor's closet, that he hit it with the machine, causing it to fly open and smack the wall.  He dumped and cleaned it, then took it up to the lobby, he kept the squeegee on again and smiled even wider as he went down the hall and down to the elevator.

He moved all the furniture to one side, and started scrubbing half the lobby.  About halfway through he stopped, walked behind the receptionist desk, used his foot to move the trashcan from under the desk, then proceeded to urinate in it, whistling while he done so. After he was done, he very carefully moved the trashcan back, then went back to scrubbing the floor.  Once done, he moved the furniture over to the other side and scrubbed the other side of the floor.  He whistled the sick jingle of his, the whole time he scrubbed.

He finally finished up the lobby and put all the furniture back. He took the machine back down, but Michelle was waiting for him when he got off the elevator. She stopped him from going any further down the hallway.

"You're gonna shut that damn machine off. I've had four residents complain so far tonight." Michelle angrily.

"They won't complain if you put a pillow over their face," Richard laughed.

"I'm going to Sheila over that comment," Michelle said and turned around to walk away then stopped and turned around "Keep the damn machine off, I know you need it on to operate, but you don't need everything else on, rude ass."

"Sir, yes, sir!" Richard said loudly and saluted Michelle, who threw her hands up as she walked away.

Richard kept the suction motor off to reduce the noise and went up the ramp and down west hall.  He stopped and opened the door to the janitor's closet, he used a doorstop to hold it open and made very little noise per Michelle's request. He drained and cleaned it out, probably better than he had ever before.

After he put the machine away, he had enough time to go reheat some coffee and enjoy a couple cups before trash run.  The west hall was rather full and at first Richard thought he was going to have to make a trip out the compactor, but east hall wasn't too bad. He would have to make a trip after that, and made sure he had his cigarettes.

He loaded up the compactor and lit a cigarette, and then turned it on.  It ran smoother than it ever had before, no shaking, no rumbling, a nice, smooth compact.  He took a long draw off the cigarette and looked at the moon, "HHHHOOOOOOOOOOOOOOOOOOOWWWWWLLLLLL!" he bellowed out at the top of his lungs, then laughed.  He took another long drag off the cigarette, then flipped it at the compactor.

Richard was bringing the cart off the elevator when Leola came up to him, "Did you hear a wolf out there?"

"Wolf? This is Indiana, ain't no wolves around here, maybe a coyote, not a wolf," Richard said in a condescending tone.

"Oh!" Leola said and felt stupid, she turned around and walked away embarrassed.

Richard went to the kitchen dock, expecting it to be a mess. It was quite the opposite, it was spotless. There was no grease on the floor, the grease can was empty and there were more trash cans, but they were only three-fourths full.  Richard easily pulled the trash out and put it in the cart.  He had finally earned some respect or had people finally done their job?

Richard took the trash out again and puffed away on another cigarette as the trash compacted.  He didn't howl at the moon this time, but he did flip his cigarette at the compactor again.  After Richard took the cart back down, he grabbed a pair of needle-nose pliers and sought out the fire extinguishers.

The first one was located ten feet from his door.  It was incased in a hard plastic, half rounded case, with white metal trim and chrome handle on the left side.  He took the fire extinguisher out and took the needle-nose pliers to the straight end of the carter pin on the handle and curled it back. This would prevent the pin from being able to be pulled out.  The next one was about halfway down west hall.  He repeated the process, then on his way to east hall, he was stopped by Leola.

"Whatchya doing?" she asked.

"Inspecting the extinguishers."

"What for?"

"Wouldn't want them malfunctioning during a fire, would we?"

"I guess not," Leola said, once again feeling stupid, she didn't like Richard, she did notice this time, his eyes were grey, but he was being so mean she didn't want to talk to him anymore.

Richard walked away and went to the fire extinguisher on east hallway, he once again repeated the process. He done the same thing with the three that were in the kitchen and the one on the loading dock.  He then went through the kitchen and traced the gas lines all around the kitchen and found a set well hidden.  He made note of them in his head.

After he left the kitchen, he made his way to the elevator room, which was right next to the elevator, in between the elevator and his office.  He looked around inside, and immediately found the shut off for the elevator.  He then went from there, to the stairwell, which was halfway between the elevator and the maintenance office. He examined the door to see if there was any way to lock it and there wasn't, so he went up to the lobby and looked and still wasn't.  He would have to find away to stop the handle from being pushed in.

He left the lobby and headed out to the shed, he unlocked it and looked in it.  The first thing that caught his attention was the axe.  He then noticed a big spool of chain, "That'll work just fine," he then looked at the axe, "I'll be seeing you tomorrow night."

Richard went back inside, but not before finishing off a cigarette.  He went to his office and got himself a cup of coffee and sat down.  He expected Leola to knock and get a cup, but she never did. He twirled around in his seats a few minutes then stopped. After the room quit spinning, he got up and went to the bathroom.  This time when he urinated it was jet black.

"Well, that's not good," he laughed and flushed the toilet.

He sat back down until it was time for the second trash run. He normally didn't go into the kitchen on the second trash run but he wanted to look at the dock doors.  He examined them, and was happy to see they could be dead bolted and he had the key for it.  He grinned at that thought, then went and took the trash out.  Leola and Michelle seemed to be avoiding him at all costs.

Once outside he made a round around the outside of building.  He noticed a three-feet high, by six-feet long and four-feet wide, green, electrical, transformer box.  It had a loud hum to it.  He knew if the power were cut from there, the back-up generator would kick in, which was located on the backside of the dome of the garden.

It ran off diesel fuel and was in a large cage to keep animals away from in.  It looked like a large diesel engine and sounded like one without an exhaust when it kicked on.  He left it alone, he wanted the backup lights to work.

He grabbed his cart and headed back inside, made some coffee.  He took a big whiff of the air, letting the nutty, robust scent fill his nose.  He poured himself a cup immediately and propped his feet up.

Soon, came time to go let Brad in.  Richard didn't say much to Brad and Brad picked up he wasn't in the mood to talk.  Brad stayed quiet as they walked to the elevator.  He didn't say anything until they got off, "Have a nice day!"

Richard gave a grumbled response and went back into his office, which he cleaned up while he was waiting for Mark to show up.  Soon came the knock that signaled the end of the shift for Richard.

Mark was wearing the work uniform and no hat this time. His lower lip had a bulge to it, which signified a chunk of chew. Richard could smell the menthol scent coming from Marks mouth, "Anything happen last night?"

"Nope, not at all, really easy night," Richard could tell by look on Mark's face, that his breath stunk.

"Well, that means today is going to be shit!" Mark said and shook his head.

Richard went back in his office to clock out, then got in his mom's car and took off.  He drove two cities over to fast food chain and ordered some biscuits and gravy, with sausage links and a side order of syrup to dip his sausage links in.  He ate everything and tossed the remnants in the back seat.

## Chapter Twenty-Three: Goodbye Maria,

## The Final Friday and Not So Final Girl

Richard drove home and when he got there, Maria was waiting on him by the front door, wearing a multi-colored, flower dress.  She had a stern look on her face.  She had her arms crossed and was tapping her left pointer finger off her right elbow.  Richard put the car and park and shut it off.  He got out and walked up to the house.

"You took the car without asking," she said.

"Did you have somewhere to go?" he asked rudely.

"It doesn't matter, you weren't supposed to take my car."

"Maybe I'm tired of riding a damned bike, I'm an adult," he said and brushed passed her.  He didn't get two steps in and Maria hit him in the back of the head with her flip flop.

"You don't talk to your momma like that. I brought you into this world and I can take you out," she said and swung a few more times, Richard put his right arm over the back of his head to stop some of the hits.

He said nothing, he tried to escape but Maria, she was relentless and finally Richard had enough.  He was by the basement door, when he turned around, grabbed her by the shoulders and screamed.  His face distorted as it turned into a mixture of Richard's and Jim's.  Maria screamed out as well, when her son's face transformed.  She screamed as he shoved her through the basement door, splintering it.  She screamed some more as she fell, but only screamed until she hit the fifth step down, which broke her neck, when she hit the tenth step down, it broke her arm. When her head hit the cinderblock wall, it fractured her skull, Maria was no more.  She was at the bottom of the steps, her extremities in all different angles, small gurgling sounds coming from her.

"Great, well can't leave her like that," Richard said himself.

He went out to the shed in the backyard and got a hacksaw and went back into the basement. He dragged Maria into the center of the basement and started to dismember her. He started with her left and right leg, he cut them just below the kneecap, the sound of the saw cutting through the bone was exhilarating. He then cut the femur off at the hip and moved to the elbow. He cut the arms off at the elbows and shoulders, then finally took the head.

He didn't have a freezer to put the body in, so he sat the torso up, then sat the arms and legs up against the torso at an angle, in a teepee like manner, he then sat her head on top of torso. There was something that wasn't sitting right with him. Maria's eyes were open and he didn't like that, he felt like she was staring at him. He walked over and put his pointer finger in one corner of her eye and his thumb in the other corner and pushed in. Her eye came out, and popped like a grape between his fingers. He repeated the process for the other eye and the same thing happened.

"That's better," he said and licked the blood from his fingers.

Richard went up to the front room after leaving the basement and sat down on the couch. He put his blood-soaked boots on the tabletop, then lit up a cigarette. As emotionless as he appeared to be about killing Maria, a single tear fell the down his left cheek. He quickly wiped it away, "That'll be enough of that crap," he said as he took a long drag off the cigarette, he let the smoke slowly roll out of his mouth, then sucked it in through his nose. He smiled as he blew the smoke back out of his mouth. After he was done smoking, he snuffed it out on the arm of the couch, then flipped the butt across the room.

He got up and went about his daily business, then went and laid down for a little bit. He didn't dream, it was just complete darkness when he shut his eyes, right until his alarm went off.

"Time to get this shit-show going," he said and went and took a nice, long, hot shower.  He wanted to leave early, because he had a surprise for Ron.

He left thirty minutes early for work, and parked in the back of the parking lot.  He walked around the perimeter of the property, keeping in the darkness of the night.  He made his way to the shed and unlocked it.  He laid his eyes upon what he was looking for, the axe.  He grabbed it then headed up the side of the building, then carefully went in through the side door.

The lobby lights were off, but Richard stayed crouched down and went behind receptionist desk.  Just as he put the axe down, the elevator dinged and for a second, Richard froze.  He heard footsteps, then heard the door jiggle.  He slightly peered up over the desk and could see Ron's back as Ron checked the door.

"Hmm, Richard is usually here by now," Ron said to himself.

It was about another ten minutes that Ron decided to walk over the desk and sit on it, "What the hell Richard?  You stinky bastard, what's taking so long?" he asked himself as he swung his feet, slightly bouncing them off the front of the desk.

Richard slowly stood up, he brought the axe up and over his head.  Quickly, he brought it down with force, sticking the blade in the back of Ron's head.  It sounded like a watermelon cracking open and blood shot out across Richard's face and the back wall.  Ron made a strange gurgling noise and when Richard pulled the axe out, Ron fell back behind the desk.  Ron had a wide, blank stare in his eyes that let Richard know, he was a goner. Richard brought the axe back up and down again, this time striking Ron in the chest. Blood poured out of Ron's mouth and out from the back of his head.  It was making its way towards Richard, Richard stepped back, his shoes had enough blood on them already.

"Now, don't be getting my shoes even more dirty!" Richard said and walked out from behind the receptionist desk and left the axe with Ron.

He went into the bathroom and washed his face and hands before he headed downstairs.  He didn't want to spoil the nights fun, by showing up with a bloody face.  He smiled in the mirror as he tossed the paper towel, he used to dry his face in the trashcan.  He then went down to his office and made a fresh pot of coffee.

While the coffee was making, he walked up and shut the curtains.  He nodded at Michelle behind the nurse's desk and at Leola as she walked by, they both were giving him odd stares.  He didn't lock the garden doors, that was his way out, there was an access ladder in the far-right corner, but made sure he locked the side door that he came through earlier.  He went back down and carried on with his normal duty and scrubbed the dining room floor.  He took the scrubber up the lobby, but didn't scrub the lobby, he simply left the scrubber up there.

Richard went back down to his office and drank a few cups of coffee, with his feet up on the desk.  He watched the monitors until it was time to do a trash run.  He took the last gulp from his coffee cup and headed down to get the cart.  Once again passing Leola, who said nothing to him, but crinkled her nose as she walked by.  The odor of rot was rampant.

Leola walked up to Michelle, "He stinks bad!"

"That boy has the devil in him, the devil is rotting his soul," Michelle said, "Let's just keep clear of him tonight, okay honey?"

"I will do my best," Leola said and watched Richard from behind the nurse's desk, he even had a different walk to him.

The west hall was overflowing with trash and Richard filled up his cart on the first haul.  He went and dumped the trash, smoked a few cigarettes, while it compacted.  He flipped his cigarette butts, grabbed the cart, and headed back down to so east hall.  It was just as bad with trash overflowing, it was another trip out to the compactor, which was fine with Richard, because that was three more cigarettes.

He figured with the trash being like it was, the kitchen trash was going to be full, but it wasn't, there were only two full bags.  He had to take them to the compactor, so he made a third round to the compactor and smoked two more cigarettes.

After the trash was done compacting, he took the cart over to the shed and grabbed the spool of chain he had seen the day before and tossed it in the cart and headed into the lobby, where he tossed the axe in the cart as well.  He opened the stairwell door and wrapped the chain around the push bar enough times that the push bar couldn't be pushed in, creating a lock for the door.  It wasn't the typical push bar, more like a push handle and he had the space to wrap the chain around the handle. He then shut the stairwell door and then pushed the scrubber in front of it, creating a block.  The chain wasn't locked with anything just tied in a knot, so if anyone were able to untie it, they still wouldn't be able to get out.

Richard went down the elevator, whistling the Jingling Jim tune as he done so.  He pushed the cart with the axe in it, down into the janitor's closet and cleaned the cart out for one last time.  He peered out the door, but decided to leave the axe in the closet for the time being and headed back outside.  He got in Maria's car and drove on the property towards the transformer.  He picked up speed and opened the door, then when he got close enough that the car wouldn't veer off course, he jumped.

The car slammed into the transformer and sparks erupted everywhere, showering Richard.  He rolled a few feet and then laid there on the cool grass a minute, face down, shielding the back of his head. He looked over and could see The Gardens was pitch black, then a loud rumble could be heard as the back up generator kicked on.  A soft, red glow came from The Gardens as the backup lights came on.

Richard got up and raced into the building, he hoped the elevator had switched over and he would be able to use it.  He was in luck, the elevator worked and when he got off of it, he could hear screaming coming from down the hall.  He raced into the elevator room and killed the power, then went down the hallway to find the source of the screaming.

"Where have you been?" Michelle asked hatefully as she jogged towards Richard from the west hall.

"I tried going up the elevator to see what went on, but the elevator is down, so I had to take the stairs.  A looney drove into the transformer box.  I've gotten ahold of the electric company they're on their way out," Richard lied through what teeth he had left.

"Everyone's going crazy, especially Mr. Latrell," Michelle said.

Richard could hear Mr. Latrell yelling, "HE HAS ARRIVED! HE HAS ARRIVED!"

Leola was going from room to room checking the residents, but most of them were still asleep. There were a few that were awake, but Leola reassured them everything was okay and they went back to bed.

Michelle ran behind the nurse's station and picked up the phone, "Phone lines are dead," she said, then grabbed her cellphone, "But we still have signal."

"Well that's because it blew up a transformer box, not a cell phone tower," Richard said and smirked.

"Now's not the time for your mouth, how long did they say before they could make it out here?" Michelle asked.

"Be a few hours," Richard said and walked away.

"Where are you going?" Michelle asked.

"I have to check the kitchen make sure nothing short-circuited, you know, so we don't blow up."

Michelle didn't say anything else as Richard walked down and into the kitchen.  He went and locked the dock doors with a smile on his face.  He looked over at the stove that housed the gas line that he had found the night before, but decided to leave it alone for the time being.

He walked back down the red, lit hallway and for the time being Leola and Michelle went about their normal duties and with them both doing paperwork, it gave Richard the time he needed to get started. He causally walked by the nurse's station and headed down west hall. He reached the cleaning room, reached inside the cart, and put his hand on the axe.

"What are you doing?" he heard Leola ask, so he let the axe go.

"Just going to clean out my cart," he replied.

"But you don't have a light," Leola pointed out.

"Well, how about you mind your own business," Richard said and even with the low, red light, he could see from the scorned look on Leola's face, she was offended.

"You're an ass!" she said and stormed off. He wanted to axe her right then and there, but he also wanted to save her for last.

He said nothing, just waited for her to turn around before grabbing onto the axe handle again. He watched as she disappeared down the hallway, then brought axe out and down to his side. He got the west master key ready and walked across the hall to the first apartment. He opened the door slowly, then quickly entered it and shut the door.

The male resident was asleep in a recliner and the T.V. was louder than what it should have been for that time of night. Richard was able sneak right up next to the resident and raise the axe above his head. The resident stirred, Richard thought they were going to wake up, but they didn't. Richard brought the axe down, square in the chest. There was a sickening crack as the axe blade broke through the sternum and a few ribs. The blade grazed the heart enough that on the next beat, it erupted. The resident just stared at Richard as the life left his eyes.

Richard pulled the axe out and blood poured out of the resident's chest, staining his blue pajamas, and soaking into the fabric of the chair. Richard smiled and watched as the blood dripped off the axe blade. Richard turned around and walked back to the door. He opened it and peeked out to see if anyone was in the hallway. He got his master key ready and hustled across to the next room. Just as he entered it, Michelle entered the hallway and looked down. She couldn't see down the hall hardly so she turned back around.

"I don't know where Richard went to, but something isn't right," Michelle said.

"Yeah, he hasn't been right at all tonight. He was nice at first, then all of sudden turned creepy," Leola said.

"I don't think he called the electric company, I'm going to call them and see if it's been reported," Michelle said and dialed the number on her cellphone, "Hello, this is Luke Energy, how may I help you," the receptionist said on the other end of the line.

"I was calling to see if a power outage has been reported at The Gardens."

"Hold for a minute and I'll take a look."

"Okay, thank you!" Michelle said and cheesy, on hold music, started to play. She was on hold about a minute before the receptionist came back on.

"There wasn't one reported according to our records, is there no power there?"

"We were told by our security that someone drove into a transformer box."

"Oh wow! We will send someone out there right away."

"Please do!" Michelle said and hung up, "I don't like the feel of this, you call 9-1-1 and go up to the lobby to let them in and stay up there."

"Okay," Leola said as she got out her phone and started heading towards the elevator, forgetting the fact it was down. She tried her badge and pressed the button a few times only to have nothing happen.

She then tried the stairwell and as she rounded the first set of steps, she stopped dead and looked at the big ball of chain on the door, "What the hell?" she asked herself as she pushed on the door only to have it not move.

While Leola was trying to get to the lobby, Michelle went down the red-lit hallway to find Richard, who was busy hacking up his second victim of the night, in their own bed. He was coming out the room, shutting the door, with the axe in front of him, when Michelle spoke up.

"I know you didn't call the electric company," she said with her right hand on her hip and her hips cocked to the side.

"I'm sure I did," Richard said, not turning around.

"I don't know what you're up to or why you're in the resident's room, but I'm calling Sheila at home and the cops," Michelle said and started to bring the phone up to here ear.

Richard grabbed the axe, spun, and swung, catching Michelle in the throat, but it was at an odd angle and the blade got stuck in Michelle's spine. Michelle's eye grew wide and she dropped her phone, shattering it. She grasped at her throat, feeling the axe head sticking out. Richard yanked the axe back out and Michelle stumbled backwards, blood gushing out of her neck wound. Richard took another swing and Michelle brought her hand up to stop it. It didn't though, the axe blade cut off four of her fingers before cutting off her head the rest of the way. Her head bounced down the hall as her body fell to its knees then, fell over forward, blood spurted out of the body and shot across Richard's shoes.

"Damnit got my shoes dirty!" he said and gave the body a little kick.

Leola had just missed Michelle's head hitting the floor as she went down east hall headed towards the dock doors.  She thought she heard something behind her, but when she turned around, she saw nothing, but red lights and dark spots down the hallway.  She couldn't see Richard but he could see her and he remained perfectly still.  He still had some axing to do, so he went into the next room.

That resident wasn't in a recliner, nor were they in bed, that's when he noticed a light on in the bathroom.  He very carefully snuck over to the side of the door.  Then brought the axe up and jumped into the doorway.  The resident was halfway through using the bathroom and her eyes got big with fear.  She managed a little scream before Richard sank the axe blade into her head.  Her eyes crossed upwards as her mouth came open.  Blood poured out of her nose and mouth and when Richard pulled the axe blade out, she slumped back.

As Richard was whacking away on west hall, Leola was in the kitchen, looking for the dock doors.  She finally found them and ran up to them only to find them locked, "No! no! no!" She said as she pushed on the push bar. "Shit!" she as she kicked the door. She knew then something bad was up.  She looked around the kitchen for something to defend herself with.  She tried the drawers but they were locked, the pots and pans were too big. All the knives that were on the magnetic strip during the day were locked up at night in a drawer.

She was about ready to give up and just hide when she kicked something with her foot. She watched as whatever it was stopped before it went under a stove. She picked it up and was about a twelve inch long, fillet knife.  She held it tightly in her and then hid in between two reach-in coolers.  It was there, she finally called 9-1-1.

"9-1-1 what's your emergency?" the dispatcher asked.

"I'm not for sure what's going on but The Gardens has no power and everything is locked, no one can get out and I think the security guard has something to do with it," Leola explained.

"Okay, so where is the security guard now?"

"I don't know he disappeared, but we can't get out and no one can get in, can you send someone to bust a window?" Leola asked as panic started to sink in.

"We will have some officers headed that way, is anybody hurt?"

"I don't know, I've been trying to find a way out and I'm hiding right now," Leola said as a loud scream broke out.  It sounded close, so Leola hung up the phone, silenced it and put it in her pocket.

Richard had made a clean sweep of west hall and was halfway down east hall when he ran into his first problem.  He entered a resident's room who was still awake and in the living room.  There was no denying Richard was there to kill him because he didn't hide the axe at all.  The resident shot up out of the chair, screamed and charged Richard, catching Richard off guard.

The resident tackled him much a football player would tackle another football player.  He drove Richard into the floor and his shoulder knocked the wind out of Richard. Richard dropped the axe in the process of the tackle.  The resident was quick for his age and strong.  He landed few good punches to Richard's face before Richard kicked him off.  The resident got up quickly and left the room. Richard was still a little dazed, but could hear the resident pounding on doors.

"GET UP! GET OUT! HE'S TRYING TO KILL US.  GET UP! GET OUT! HE'S TRYING TO KILL US," the resident yelled as he went to the few remaining doors.

 He was on his last door getting ready to knock when Richard launched the axe through the air.  The blade of the axe stuck squarely in between the shoulder blades of the resident.  The resident tried to reach behind himself to pull the axe out, but he couldn't reach. He fell to his knees and Richard walked up to him, put his foot on the resident's back, then pushed it forward as Richard pulled the axe out.

The resident's head bounced off the doorframe, then the resident fell off to the side.

He didn't waste any time finishing off the rest of east hall. They were all too feeble to fight back and one hit, done them in. Just about every resident in The Gardens was dead and Richard headed towards the kitchen. He didn't know where Leola was, but he knew she couldn't escape, and he had other things to worry about.

Mr. Latrell had heard the chaos and was actually in the right state of mind to get himself in the wheelchair. He slightly cracked his door and looked out just in time to see Michelle's head fall onto the floor. He looked over and Richard was staring down the hall at something.

Mr. Latrell froze in fear, but managed to start praying. The crack in his door that was filled with red light, darkened, he thought for sure he was going to meet his maker. He shut his eyes, expecting Richard to kick his door open. It didn't happen though, Richard was distracted and it worked out in Mr. Latrell's favor.

Mr. Latrell wheeled his way his to closet and opened the door. He moved some stuff around on the floor and pulled out a box that he kept hidden for a long time. He reached down, grabbed the worn out, cardboard box and lifted it up. In the box, long hidden, was his robe, collar, rosaries, and a crucifix. The crucifix was a special one, not only was it silver, but it had a blade built into it. He only had to use it a few times before, and always regretted it afterwards. He wasn't going to regret it this time.

Richard entered the kitchen, he went to the gas lines he spotted the night before. Richard knew he needed a wrench or channel locks to get the gas lines off and maintenance probably had some. He didn't want to use the axe for fear of causing a spark. He turned around and Leola watched him from in between the coolers. She waited until she heard the kitchen doors shut to get out from her hiding spot.

She decided to try the garden area, but she wanted to see where Richard went with the axe.  So she peered around the corner and watched as Richard made a right.  She stayed low until she got to the corner of the main hall and east hall and looked around the corner.  Richard wasn't in sight, so she stood up and ran to the garden.  She never really went in there, so she didn't know if there was an exit door or a way to open the windows and get out.  She searched frantically, climbing behind the bushes and plants, trying to find any opening she could, but there was nothing she could see, in a panic she overlooked the access ladder. She went to a window that she could reach and tried prying at it with the fillet knife.  She couldn't get the knife to go into the seal, so she was going to have to try the dock doors again.

While she was searching, Richard made his way back down to the kitchen with some channel locks.  He shut the gas valve off and then took the fitting off the back of the stove with channel locks.  Afterwards he turned the gas valve about halfway on, letting gas leak out into the kitchen.  He then found a couple of metal spoons, just the right length to fit in the microwave, across the room.  He walked over to the microwave and put the spoons in, pressed the defrost button and put it on for forty-minutes then hit start.  He heard them sparking before he even left the kitchen.

He was going to go wait in the garden, he didn't care where Leola was at, she couldn't have gotten out, so once the kitchen blew, she'd perish with everyone else.  As he was passing the dining room, he heard tapping on glass.  It was coming from the dining room or so he thought.  Once he got in the dining room, he realized it was coming from the garden. He peeked through the curtains and at first didn't see anything, then he saw the source of the tapping.  It was Leola and she was using the knife to try to pry at the seal of a window.

"Guess I'm gonna get to kill that broad after all," he smiled and hurried down to the garden.

Leola was walking towards the garden doors, she turned to look back and noticed there were red and blue lights reflecting off the windows of the dome, the cops must have showed up. Then, when she turned back around, there stood Richard, with the axe down by his side.  The red light from the emergency light was hitting him on the top of his face, highlighting his nose, but darkening his eyes.  She could see an evil smile on his face.

"I see your friends arrived, but they won't be able to get in and even if they do, this place is going to go boom!" Richard said and smiled.

She brought the knife up Richard could see it, "Just let me go."

"Nah," Richard said and waited, he expected Leola to act, but she didn't, "I think I'd rather sink this axe in the front of your skull," he said, bringing the axe up and twirling it.  Then, before she could say anything, Richard lunged, and Leola dove off to the side, the axe barely missed her.

She scrambled to get to her feet and when she did, she saw the axe coming for her again, and had to dive again.  This time she landed near the steps that led up to the catwalk over the pond. Richard lunged again, this time Leola ducked and rammed the knife into Richard's gut.  He moaned out in pain and took a few steps back, still holding onto the axe, which he, shortly after being stabbed, dropped.  He looked down at the knife sticking out of his stomach. He looked back at Leola and smiled as blood dripped out if his mouth.

"I think it'll be much more fun," he said, then pulled the knife out of his stomach, "taking your face off with this."

Leola turned to climb up the steps of the catwalk and Richard was on her before she could think.  He stuck knife through her hand, she screamed and out of instinct, she back elbowed him in the face, which caused him to fall off to the side.  She got up and grabbed her right hand with her left hand and looked at the knife handle, then slowly turned her hand so she could see the blade of the knife sticking out the front of her hand.

"Ohhhhh mmyyyyy goddddd!" she said as blood dripped from the wound.

"God has nothing to do with it," Richard said and felt his jaw where she elbowed him.

"Why are you doing this?" Leola asked.

"I started this a long time ago and I'm here to finish it.  I was stopped last time, I won't be stopped this time," Richard said.

"What are you talking about Richard?"

"Don't you know girl," Richard said, pulling his keys out and jingling them, "Richards gone, I'm Jingling Jim McCurdy."

Richard ran towards Leola and started screaming, there was nowhere for her to go being on the catwalk, so she done the only thing she could think of.  She swung at Richard with the knife-hand. It caught him in the side of the throat, but it did not slow his momentum.  He picked up Leola and they fell over the back railing of the catwalk.  They hit sideways on the top of the waterfall, the knife blade tore through Richard's throat as Leola fell off the side of the waterfall, she somehow went face first onto the concrete floor.  Her jaw shattered upon impact and so did a few teeth.

After a minute of not moving, she rolled over on her back, turned her head sideways and spit out some blood and teeth. Pain shot through face and mouth.  She looked up and Richard was on top of the of the waterfall, on his back, his head almost decapitated, looking right at Leola.  Blood trickled down and out of his open mouth, and over his eyes.

Leola laid there a minute, the pain in her jaw was unbearable. She rolled over and pushed herself up with one hand, blood pouring from her mouth.  She brought her injured hand up to her side and used her left hand and leg strength to stand.  She looked up at Richard but he wasn't there.  She started to panic and limped towards the garden doors.

Richard felt his head start to reattach and when Leola rolled over to spit out a mouthful of blood and teeth, he fell into the pond. He saw the fillet knife reflecting off the redlight and reached for it.

He slowly raised his head above water, and Leola was gone. He could hear her shuffling and slowly moved to the edge of the pond. He watched as she headed out the door and back into the hallway. He crawled out of the pond, what bones that were broken were popping back in place as he crawled across the floor.

Mr. Latrell heard screaming coming from the garden and he looked out his window and watched as Leola and Richard fell off the catwalk. He thought for sure Leola was dead, but a surge of hope coursed through him when she started to move. He also watched as Richard's dangling head pulled up closer to his body. He tried pounding on the window, but in his feeble state, he could barely make an audible noise. He watched as Leola limped to the double doors of the garden. He rolled to his door and pulled himself up, he cracked the door and waited.

Leola was limping as fast as she could, when suddenly she was yanked to the side. She had a hand put over her mouth and Mr. Latrell was tell her to shush. He removed his hand, "Shush child, he's coming!"

They both stared through the crack in the door as Richard came out of the garden doors. The red light from the emergency light was shining in Richard's eyes, he couldn't see as he walked by Mr. Latrell's room. Mr. Latrell waited until Richard was a few feet away and opened his door. In an untimely manner, the door squeaked, but in a burst of energy, Mr. Latrell found his leg strength and shot forwards, the crucifix knife raised above his head.

Richard brought up the fillet knife as Mr. Latrell brought the crucifix knife down. Richard plunged the knife upwards, under Mr. Latrell's ribs and right into his heart. Mr. Latrell brought his knife down, through Richard's chest right into his heart. The two locked eyes for a brief second, Mr. Latrell fell back and Richard let out a shriek.

Richard's body shot back, arms and legs popping and going in all angles. He got down on all fours, but backwards and ran down the hall, plowing into the wall and falling over. Leola limped as fast as she could towards Richard who was laying in heap of twisted body parts by the time she got to him.  She forced him on his back and pulled the knife out of his chest.  She raised the knife above her head with both hands on it.

"Leola...waits...its me..Richard!" Richard said and held out his hand.

Leola was having none of it, she plunged the knife into Richard's head and black ooze formed around where the knife and skull met.  Richard's hand dropped and the nightmare of Jingling Him and Richard Ruiz was over.

She took his keys and got up, painfully, slowly and headed back up to the stairs next to the elevator.  It took everything she had to make it up the steps to the chained door.  She fumbled around with the chain, then  finally unraveled it and tried to open the door, the scrubber wasn't budging on the other side.

Leola tried to scream but all that came out was a high pitch whine of a scream.  The door opened enough that Leola could see the cops on the outside of the building.

While Leola was messing with door, the microwave exploded, in the forty-minutes it took for the microwave to go off, the room filled up with the gas. The explosion ripped through The Gardens, destroying everything in sight, and then raced up the stairs. The force of the explosion shoved the scrubber over and forced Leola out of the door. It singed the back part of Leola, scrubs, hair and skin.  She landed in the lobby and slid.  Everything behind the stairwell door collapsed, the large glass windows in front exploded, sending shards of glass over the cops and paramedics that were outside.

The cops ducked behind their cars and waited a few seconds before raising their heads to look.  At first there wasn't any movement coming from what was left of the lobby, then some rubble moved.  Leola managed, once again, to pull herself up one handed. The cops shone their lights on her as she made her way out front. She used the hand with the keys in it to shield the light from her eyes.

"SHE'S GOT A WEAPON!" one of the officers yelled.

"DROP THE WEAPON!" another officer yelled.

Leola couldn't talk on the account of her jaw being broken. All she could do was cry and mumble as blood came out of her mouth.  She walked around the fountain, slowly, with her hand up, attempting to show the officers that the keys was in her hand.

"STOP, DROP THE WEAPON OR WE WILL SHOOT!" another officer said.

She tried pointing to the keys and took another step forward. That's when a shot rang out, hitting Leola in the shoulder, then another shot and another.  Finally, a shot rang out, and the bullet hit her right between the eyes. She fell straight back into the fountain. Her blood tainted the water and blood water poured out of the statue's mouth.  Red and blue lights flashed off Leola's face as the life slipped out of her.

# Chapter Twenty-Four: The Aftermath

Hours after the incident a clean-up crew came in and that's when they found the real horror of what happened.  It took clean-up crews four days to get all the bodies out of The Gardens rubble.  They found the axe and matched the fingerprints on them to be Richards and pinned his death on Leola.

The officers somehow spun a story that Richard and Leola were in it together and she turned on Richard.  The media blew up with the story and it made national news. Yertsville was famous once again.

Four months after the massacre Mr. Helsir ordered the rest of The Gardens to be demolished, but saved the roses from the garden. He watched from the comfort of his limousine, with the window slightly cracked and a cane in his hand.  He watched as a dozer pushed through what was left of the lobby and as a group of men took out what windows were left in the garden area.

"So what's next Mr. Helsir?" the driver asked from the front seat.

"There is nothing here, I'll own this property until I die, so no one will be able to rebuild The Gardens.  I believe my father got what he was looking for," Mr. Helsir said and smiled.

"Yeah, but it couldn't have been done without so much death?" the driver asked and looked in the mirror.

"What fun would that have been?" Mr. Helsir laughed then tapped the floor with his cane, "Let's get a move on, they're taking the incinerator out of here and taking it to my house, a collectible if you will. Anyways, this is just one of thirteen other facilities I own and they all have their lovely backstory that, with a little prompting, could come back to haunt them."

"You are a strange one Mr. Helsir."

"That I am, but I do pay good."

"Yes, sir you do!" the driver laughed.

Mr. Helsir rolled up his window and drove away.  He never set foot in Yerzville again, and the story of Jingling Jim was replaced the story of Richard "Ramirez" Ruiz.